Vegan Casseroles

Vegan Casseroles

Pasta Bakes, Gratins, Pot Pies, and More

JULIE HASSON

RUNNING PRESS
PHILADELPHIA · LONDON

Books published by Running Press are available at special discounts for bulk purchases in the United States by corporations, institutions, and other organizations. For more information, please contact the Special Markets Department at the Perseus Books Group, 2300 Chestnut Street, Suite 200, Philadelphia, PA 19103, or call (800) 810-4145, ext. 5000, or e-mail special.markets@perseusbooks.com.

ISBN 978-0-7624-4884-5
Library of Congress Control Number: 2013951598
E-book ISBN 978-0-7624-5528-7

9 8 7 6 5 4 3 2 1
Digit on the right indicates the number of this printing

Cover and interior design by Jason Kayser
Edited by Kristen Green Wiewora
Typography: Celias and Freight

Running Press Book Publishers
2300 Chestnut Street
Philadelphia, PA 19103–4371

Visit us on the web!
www.offthemenublog.com

To Jay, Sydney, and Noah,
the loves of my life.
How did I ever get so lucky?

CONTENTS

ACKNOWLEDGMENTS

◆ ◆ ◆

First and foremost, thank you, Jay. You are truly my other half and my best friend, and you make every day a fun adventure. I love you to the moon and back!

A giant thank-you to my incredible children, Sydney and Noah. You guys are the best! Your taste-testing, recipe suggestions, and never-ending patience while I was "buried" in the kitchen are bar none. I love you guys!

I also want to thank everyone involved with putting this book together. Lisa and Sally Ekus, my stellar super-agents: it's always a pleasure working with you two. Kristen Green Wiewora, my editor at Running Press, for helping this book come together so beautifully. Felicia Perretti for your stellar photos, Lori Lewis and Katie Wilson for your great proofreading and copyediting, and designer Jason Kayser for making this book look so cool.

Mom, thank you for so many things, but especially for introducing me to tofu, home-cooked dinners, and homemade bread, all those years ago. You taught me what real food is all about, and I will be forever grateful. And Jon, what can I say? You are not only the best brother a girl could ever have, but there is no one else that I can talk food with like we do. Dad and Ellen, thank you for your love and support, and for sharing my cookbooks with everyone you meet.

A big thank-you to Bob's Red Mill, Ancient Harvest Pasta, Sweet & Sara Marshmallows, Beyond Meat, and Butler Foods for letting me test recipes with your fantastic products! And last but not least, thank you to my wonderful crew of taste testers, who so enthusiastically tested out these recipes and always gave me your honest feedback: Craig Lee, Jill Russell, Thalia Palmer, Marti Miller Hall, Kelly Cavalier, Rebekah Reid, Susan Gottlieb, Brandie Britt, Krys Kagan, Sheree Britt, Matt, and James.

INTRODUCTION

◆ ◆ ◆

Just mention the word "casserole," and you can see people's faces light up. Casseroles evoke associations of comfort food and warm, family meals, and favorite dishes that mothers or grandmothers served for dinner. Casseroles are a classic dish often brought to church gatherings, potlucks, and even weddings! Big dishes of layered creamy goodness and love, and are always welcome at my table.

Casseroles are the epitome of one-dish meals, which became very popular in the United States in the 1950s. All of those TV moms of yore would don their stylish aprons and serve piping-hot casseroles to their hungry, happy families.

Traditionally, casseroles are made with modern convenience foods like canned soup, frozen vegetables and potatoes, a multitude of seasonings, and copious amounts of butter, cheese, and meat. They are definitely not healthy but are certainly tasty.

So when I set out to write this book, I thought it would be pretty easy to take traditional casserole recipes and give them a vegan spin. Wow: I couldn't have been more wrong. Even though grocery stores are now filled to the brim with all sorts of vegan analogues and versions of traditional staples like meat, cheese, sour cream, cream cheese, and milk, you can't just swap vegan ingredients for their non-vegan counterparts. Seriously, trust me on this. I also discovered that, although a lot of the original casseroles are delicious, I couldn't, in good conscience, feel okay about adding two sticks of vegan butter to a dish and calling it "done," no matter how buttery and good it might taste. So I had to rethink the whole casserole concept and look at it with fresh eyes.

This was no easy task. For starters, one of the best things about casseroles is how quickly you can throw them together. So if you're not relying on packaged, store-bought, prepared foods, how do you make a casserole with all of its components in under three hours? This was the biggest challenge of all, but I was determined to have the recipes come together easily. So I created a whole chapter of sauces that are quickly mixed in the blender and then cooked on the stove top. These sauces are easily mixed with your casserole components, such as cooked pasta, rice, quinoa, potatoes, or veggies. The sauce chapter is key, because the sauces are truly what give the casseroles their great taste and creamy texture, and bind everything together. And there's no need for canned condensed soups anymore, because I've got a fresh take covered in the book too, which might be perfect for veganizing Aunt Betty's Thanksgiving green bean casserole. Frozen spinach, hash browns, and beloved potato tots are pretty much the only frozen ingredients you'll find in the recipes. Although you could make those from scratch, I'm trying to save you from spending the entire day in the kitchen. Remember, these are modern, streamlined casseroles.

I didn't want to only include American-style casseroles, so there's also lots of international casserole favorites too, like lasagna, enchiladas, stuffed cabbage rolls, kugels, stove-top casseroles, desserts, and so much more.

These casseroles are much healthier than traditional casseroles. No cholesterol, no animal products, and definitely no gobs of cheese and butter. These are casseroles that you can truly feel good serving to your family, without any guilt.

Although most of the recipes in this book are baked in an 8-inch square baking dish and serve 4, many of the recipes can be doubled. Casseroles are meant to serve a crowd, should the need arise.

I hope that you enjoy these recipes, and, just like those 1950s TV moms, make them a regular part of your dinner routine. Of course, don't stop there. These dishes are perfect for potlucks, big gatherings, and anytime you need to bring a dish that will make everyone feel warm and loved.

Flavorings and Seasonings

Bragg: Also known as Bragg liquid aminos. It is made from soybeans and has a taste that is similar to soy sauce. Look for Bragg in well-stocked health-food stores.

Canned Chipotle Peppers: Red ripe jalapeños that have been slow smoked and canned in adobo sauce. Chipotles have a deep, smoky flavor.

Liquid Smoke: Liquid smoke adds a wonderfully smoky flavor to recipes. It is in fact vegan and natural, but check the ingredient label because some varieties add dyes and additives.

Nutritional Yeast Flakes: Dried flakes derived from yeast are high in B vitamins, protein, and minerals. Nutritional yeast also acts as a flavor enhancer in food. I especially love Red Star brand nutritional yeast flakes.

Poultry Seasoning: A must-use spice blend in the vegan kitchen! This is a savory blend of herbs and spices, which typically includes thyme, sage, marjoram, rosemary, black pepper, and nutmeg.

Salt: All of the recipes in this book were tested with fine sea salt.

Smoked Paprika: Also known as pimentón or Spanish paprika. When used in cooking, it imparts a wonderful smoky flavor to food.

Tamari: Tamari soy sauce is made from soybeans. Sometimes it's made with a little wheat, and sometimes with no wheat at all. If you're gluten-free, look for tamari that is specifically labeled gluten-free.

Vegan Bouillon: Vegan bouillon paste, powder, and cubes are great for flavoring casseroles, sauces, Soy Curls, and more. Two of my favorites for using in casseroles are Better Than Bouillon No Beef Base and No Chicken Base. They have an awesome flavor. I also love Knorr Funghi Porcini cubes, which are imported from Italy. Always check the ingredients to make sure they are vegan. Harvest 2000® Vegetarian Chicken Flavor Bouillon Powder is another good-tasting vegan chicken bouillon. Each brand varies in saltiness, so add to taste. They are usually available in well-stocked grocery and health-food stores or online.

Flours, Thickeners, Sweeteners, and Baking Aids

Chocolate: Look for dairy-free varieties of dark and semisweet chocolate and chocolate chips. Many brands are now fair trade and organic too.

Cocoa Powder: Look for Dutch process, which is a dark, rich cocoa powder processed with alkali, which neutralizes its natural acidity.

Cornstarch: A thickening agent made from corn. Look for organic or non-GMO varieties.

Margarine: Look for a good-tasting, vegan, nondairy, nonhydrogenated margarine such as Earth Balance® brand. Margarine can be used almost interchangeably when a recipe calls for butter, especially when a buttery taste is required.

Oat Flour: If you're gluten-free, look for certified gluten-free oat flour, which can be found in well-stocked grocery or health-food stores or online. I especially like the wonderful flours from Bob's Red Mill and used their flours for testing the recipes in this book. If you can't find oat flour, you can also grind rolled oats into flour

using a blender, although it's hard to get it quite as fine as the store-bought (which is what you want for a silky sauce).

Oil: I generally use canola oil for baking and olive oil for cooking. I find that not only does canola oil have a mild flavor, but cakes actually come out softer and fluffier. Both oils come in organic varieties. If you're looking to reduce the fat in the recipes, you can use cooking spray instead of oil for sautéing and roasting.

Potato Starch: For gluten-free baking, I like to use potato starch in combination with other gluten-free flours. It contributes a nice soft crumb and texture. It can also be used as a thickener for sauces, soups, and stews.

Sorghum Flour: Sorghum is a millet-like cereal grain, which is milled into a soft, fine, gluten-free flour. It is a powerhouse of nutrition and adds a superb flavor to gluten-free baking. My favorite is the Sweet White Sorghum Flour from Bob's Red Mill or Authentic Foods. If you can't eat gluten-free oats, you can substitute an equal amount of sorghum flour for the oat flour in the sauce recipes.

Sugar: Not all sugars are vegan, as cane sugar is sometimes filtered through bone char (from animals). Beet sugar (granulated white and brown) and organic sugars are processed without the use of bone char.

Superfine Brown Rice Flour: Superfine brown rice flour is the best rice flour to use for gluten-free baking. There's no grittiness whatsoever, as there can be with regular rice flour. It's definitely worth seeking this flour out, which is made by Authentic Foods.

Sweet White Rice Flour: Sweet white rice flour is made from high-starch, short-grain rice and is very different from regular rice flour. Please note that sweet white rice flour is definitely not interchangeable with regular rice flour. Sweet white rice flour is what binds everything together in Italian Stuffed Peppers with Fennel and Garlic (page 139) and Italian-Style Stuffed Swiss Chard (page 112). There can be a big difference between brands of sweet white rice flour, as I discovered during recipe testing. The two brands that I found work best are Bob's Red Mill and Authentic Foods. The sweet white rice flour from Asian markets doesn't work as well in these recipes, as it can be too gummy.

Tapioca Starch/Flour: Tapioca starch is a starch extracted from the cassava root, and it is completely gluten-free. Not all brands of tapioca flour/starch are created equal. I find that some brands of tapioca starch can have an off flavor, and some vary in their absorption capabilities. My favorite go-to brands of tapioca starch are Authentic Foods and Shiloh Farms.

Unbleached All-Purpose Flour: When I call for regular wheat flour in some of the recipes, I find that they come out best with unbleached all-purpose flour.

Vanilla: Always use pure vanilla, never artificial! I use and love the vanilla from Nielsen-Massey. They also carry a vanilla paste, which is incredible, with little flecks of the vanilla bean.

Xanthan Gum: Xanthan gum is used to add volume and viscosity to gluten-free baked goods. It can also be used as a thickener.

Proteins, Milks, and Cheeses

Soymilk: Milk made from soybeans. Look for organic varieties if possible. You will notice that I primarily use unsweetened plain soymilk in the sauce recipes. I tried making the recipes with a number of other nondairy milks, but I had the best results with the unsweetened soy. By far, it adds the richest, creamiest texture to the sauces.

Tofu: Made from soymilk and is a high-quality source of protein. Tofu comes in many different varieties, from silken to extra-firm. Silken is usually best blended in desserts, dressings, or creamy sauces. I like the Mori-Nu brand.

TSP or TVP Granules: Textured soy protein or textured vegetable protein (both are essentially the same thing). It's made from defatted soy flour. It's low in fat and high in protein, and it cooks quickly. Look for organic TSP. The brand I usually use is Bob's Red Mill.

Vegan Cheese: There are several brands of vegan cheese that melt and will work beautifully in your casseroles, should you want them to be cheesy. There's Daiya, GO Veggie!, Follow Your Heart, and Teese, with more companies sure to come. You can also eliminate the vegan cheese from the recipes altogether. It's totally your call.

Vegan Chicken: Vegan chicken is a great way to add more protein and bulk to your casseroles. There are several varieties of vegan chicken available, although currently there are only a couple of products that are gluten-free (if that's how you roll). Make sure to check the ingredient list if you are unsure. Here are a few favorites:

Beyond Meat: Gluten-free and made from soy and pea protein, Beyond Meat vegan chicken strips are fully cooked and can be stirred right into the casserole filling.

Gardein: Gardein is not gluten-free; it is made from wheat and soy proteins. It is also fully cooked and can be added directly to the unbaked casserole filling.

Seitan: Feel free to use diced homemade or store-bought seitan in the recipes too. Seitan is made from vital wheat gluten, and it has a nice, chewy texture. It is not gluten-free.

Soy Curls: A delicious and versatile product made from whole, non-GMO soybeans. These come in dried strips and simply need to be reconstituted in hot broth or water for 10 minutes. They are available online and in some health-food stores.

Vegan Cream Cheese and Sour Cream: There are a couple of brands of vegan, nondairy cream cheese and sour cream now on the market. My first choice is Tofutti, which is what I used for testing recipes in this book. I like Follow Your Heart brand too, which also makes a delicious mayonnaise called Vegenaise.

Special Equipment

Baking Dishes: Although I call for glass or ceramic baking dishes in the recipes, you could also use enameled cast iron too. I would suggest not using metal cake pans, as they can cause the casserole to bake faster and hotter. When I call for a certain size baking dish, you can substitute a similar size casserole dish. Just know that the baking times might change slightly if you change the size or dimensions of the dish.

8-inch square baking dish = 2-quart casserole dish
11 x 7-inch baking dish = 2-quart casserole dish
9-inch square baking dish = 2 ½-quart casserole dish
13 x 9-inch baking dish = 3-quart casserole dish

Cast-Iron Skillet: I love cast-iron skillets and use mine whenever I need to sauté: plus, you can bake right in the same skillet. If you regularly season your pan, it becomes almost nonstick. My favorites are the seasoned cast-iron pans from Lodge. They're inexpensive, work amazingly well, and will last forever.

Dry Metal Measuring Cups: This is the most accurate way to measure dry ingredients (with the exception of a digital scale), and what I always use to measure my flour. Always spoon your flour or other dry ingredients into the cup and level the top by scraping across with the flat side of a knife (or a skewer). This will give you an accurate measurement.

Liquid Measuring Cups: The most accurate way to measure liquid ingredients is in glass or plastic liquid measuring cups with a lip or spout. I like to keep a variety of different sizes in my kitchen for baking.

Metal Measuring Spoons: This is the most accurate way to measure small amounts of both liquid and dry ingredients.

Microplane Zester/Grater: A handy tool for quickly removing and grating citrus zest. It also works well for grating cinnamon sticks, whole nutmeg, garlic, and ginger.

Mixing Bowls: A nesting set (or two or three) of mixing bowls is a must in the kitchen. I like to have both stainless steel and ceramic, depending on the mixing job.

Whisk: A great tool for whipping or whisking both liquid and dry ingredients. I like to use it to mix together and aerate dry ingredients in recipes, as well as to emulsify dressings and sauces.

Silicone Spatulas: The new silicone spatulas are heatproof to 600°F (316°C). They are a boon to cooks, as they will scrape a bowl clean with ease. They are dishwasher-safe and can be used for stove-top cooking as well.

Blender: This really helps in the casserole kitchen, from blending cashews into a silken cream to whipping silken tofu into a luscious sauce. In fact, I use the blender for most of the sauces in this book. High-speed blenders really do work best, especially when making sauces with cashews. There are several brands that I have used and loved over the years, including the well-known Vitamix and Blendtec's Total Blender models. Power and wattage does make a difference when it comes to a blender.

Food Processor: This machine is essential for chopping vegetables and nuts, blending tofu, and a million other things! I recommend the Cuisinart or KitchenAid brands, as they will last for years and do a more consistent job than less expensive brands.

Immersion/Stick Blender: I love immersion blenders. They blend ingredients quickly with a minimum of mess. They are great for blending canned tomatoes right in the can. There are many brands, including Cuisinart and KitchenAid.

Oven: What matters most here is that you make sure that your oven is calibrated (precisely adjusted) so that it bakes evenly and at the required temperature. I also recommend using an oven thermometer, so that you know what temperature your oven is actually reaching. The recipes in this book were tested using a conventional gas oven.

Helpful Casserole Tips and Tricks

- Read the entire recipe through before starting. This way you know both the steps and the ingredients in the recipe before you begin.

- Make sure that your oven is properly preheated before baking. It will probably take 10 to 15 minutes to preheat, depending on your oven.

- When measuring dry ingredients, always spoon your dry ingredients into dry metal measuring cups or spoons, and level the top by scraping across it with the flat side of a knife (or a skewer).

- For best results, use glass, ceramic, or stoneware baking dishes.

- You should always check the casserole 5 minutes before its minimum recommended cooking time. Each oven bakes differently.

- When using aluminum foil to cover your casserole, put the shiny side down, as it can reflect the heat.

- Cook a big pot of brown rice, quinoa, or other grain at one time, so that you have leftovers to use for last-minute casseroles or quick weeknight meals. The same goes for cooking beans too. Both cooked grains and beans can be frozen as well.

- Have fun!

Casserole Topping Suggestions

Looking for a crispy, crunchy casserole topping? You can top any of the casseroles with your choice of the following toppings:

- Crushed potato chips
- Crushed crisp rice cereal like Rice Chex (plus, it's gluten-free)
- Crushed rice cakes
- Panko breadcrumbs (regular or gluten-free)
- Crushed crackers
- Buttery Crumb Topping (page 162)
- Toasted waffle crumbs

Chapter One

...

One-Dish
Appetizers

Baked Tapenade

This recipe is a fun twist on traditional tapenade, and it makes a fantastic appetizer. Serve it with some wonderful rustic bread, crostini, or crackers.

Makes about 1 cup

2 cloves garlic
1 cup pitted Kalamata olives
2 tablespoons drained capers
2 tablespoons olive oil
¼ teaspoon crushed dried thyme

Preheat the oven to 350°F. Grease a very small baking dish, such as 8 x 5 inches, or a small cast-iron skillet.

Finely chop the garlic in a food processor. Add the olives, capers, olive oil, and thyme to the food processor and process until finely chopped.

Transfer the olive mixture to the prepared dish and bake for 15 to 20 minutes, or until the tapenade is warm. Serve right away.

Gluten-Free: Serve with gluten-free crackers.

Mushroom and Caramelized Onion Pâté

Sometimes it's fun to do a more elegant twist on a casserole, and this is one of those recipes. It can be assembled earlier in the day and refrigerated until ready to serve.

Serves 4 as an appetizer

1 tablespoon olive oil

5 cups sliced cremini or brown mushrooms, rinsed and patted dry

1 large yellow onion, thinly sliced

2 teaspoons granulated sugar

1 cup raw walnuts or pecans

2 tablespoons Marsala or brandy

2 teaspoons nutritional yeast flakes

1 teaspoon fine sea salt, or more to taste

Freshly ground black pepper to taste

1 teaspoon minced fresh rosemary leaves, or ¼ teaspoon dried, plus 1 sprig for garnish

In a large skillet, heat the oil over medium-high heat. Add the mushrooms and onions, and sauté until the onions are softening and becoming translucent. Sprinkle the sugar over the mushroom mixture and continue to cook until the onions are caramelized, for about 15 minutes, reducing the heat as necessary so that the onions don't burn. Remove the skillet from the heat.

In the bowl of a food processor fitted with the metal blade, pulse the nuts until they are finely chopped. Add the mushroom mixture and blend until the mixture is smooth. Add the Marsala, nutritional yeast, and salt and pepper to taste. Gently pulse in the rosemary, being careful not to purée it too finely.

Spread the pâté into an 8-inch square glass or ceramic baking dish, or four to six individual ramekins. Place a sprig of fresh rosemary on top.

Serve with crackers or toasted bread slices.

Caramelized Onion Dip

This dip is adapted from a recipe by Dan and Annie Shannon in *Betty Goes Vegan*. No one will ever guess that it's not full of sour cream, but heart-healthy creamy cashews instead. I doubled the onion-y goodness with dried chopped onion, which will totally remind you of the quintessential French onion dip. Serve this old-school style, with ruffled potato chips on the side. Prepare to be wowed!

Serves 8

2 cups raw unsalted cashews, soaked for at
    least 2 hours and drained
½ cup white wine
½ cup warm water
2 tablespoons freshly squeezed lemon juice
1 clove garlic, pressed or finely minced
1 tablespoon granulated onion
1 tablespoon plus 1 teaspoon Bragg liquid
    aminos or low-sodium tamari or soy sauce
Fine sea salt to taste
2 tablespoons dried chopped onion
1 tablespoon olive oil
1 jumbo or 2 small sweet onions, cut into
    quarters and thinly sliced
A few pinches granulated sugar

In a powerful blender, combine the cashews, wine, water, lemon juice, garlic, granulated onion, and Bragg liquid aminos. Blend until the mixture is super-smooth and creamy, and there are no traces of graininess from the nuts. This will take a couple of minutes, and you will need to stop to scrape down the blender jar. Adjust seasonings to taste, adding salt if needed.

Scoop the cashew mixture into a small glass or ceramic baking dish, such as an 8 x 5 or 8½ x 6 (or you can use a standard loaf pan). Stir in the dried onions and smooth the top. Cover and chill for several hours.

While the cashew mixture is chilling, heat a large cast-iron skillet over medium heat. Add the oil, coating the bottom of the pan. Add the onions and cook for about 30 minutes, stirring as needed, until the onions are caramelized. You may need to lower the heat so that the onions don't burn. During the last 10 minutes of cooking, sprinkle the onions with a few pinches of sugar and a pinch of salt to help them caramelize. When the onions are soft and nicely browned, remove them from the heat and let cool completely.

(recipe continues)

When the dip has chilled and thickened for several hours, top with the caramelized onions and serve.

Tip: If you're using a high-speed blender, you can skip the soaking step for the cashews and just use them dry. Add a little extra water to blend if needed.

Variation: To add an extra onion flavor to the dip, and a little splash of color, sprinkle a handful of thinly sliced scallions over the caramelized onions.

Gluten-Free: Use gluten-free tamari or gluten-free soy sauce.

Five-Layer Hummus Dip

I needed to make a fun dip for a birthday party one night, and I came up with this new twist on the classic seven-layer taco dip, full of fresh Mediterranean flavors. The dip can be made earlier in the day and refrigerated until ready to serve. The Creamy Dill Sauce is adapted from an awesome recipe from vegan cookbook author Sarah Kramer.

Serves 4 as an appetizer

HUMMUS

1 (15-ounce) can chickpeas, drained
    and rinsed (1½ cups)
¼ cup cool water
2 tablespoons freshly squeezed lemon juice
¼ cup roasted tahini
2 large cloves garlic
1 teaspoon ground cumin
2 teaspoons toasted sesame oil

CREAMY DILL SAUCE

1 (10-ounce) box firm or extra-firm silken
    tofu (such as Mori-Nu)
2 tablespoons raw unsalted cashews, soaked for
    at least 2 hours and drained
1 large clove garlic
1 teaspoon fine sea salt
1 teaspoon granulated onion
3 tablespoons cool water
1 tablespoon dried dill

TOPPINGS

2 large Roma tomatoes, finely diced
About ½ to ⅔ cup sliced, pitted Kalamata olives
5 scallions, thinly sliced

FOR THE HUMMUS

In the jar of a powerful blender or a food processor, combine the chickpeas, water, lemon juice, tahini, garlic, cumin, and sesame oil. Blend until the hummus is smooth, adding more water a little at a time if needed. Transfer the hummus to a small baking dish (about 8½ x 6 inches or an 8- or 9-inch glass loaf pan), spreading the hummus into an even layer. Cover and refrigerate the dish while you make the next layer. Rinse and dry the blender jar to make the sauce.

FOR THE SAUCE

In a powerful blender, combine the tofu, cashews, garlic, salt, granulated onion, and water. Blend until the sauce is very smooth and there aren't any trace bits of nuts. If the sauce is too thick to blend, you can add another tablespoon of water. Add the dill and blend just until mixed. Carefully spread the sauce over the hummus layer in the baking dish. Cover and refrigerate until right before serving.

FOR THE TOPPINGS

Right before serving, sprinkle the diced tomatoes over the sauce. If the tomatoes are really juicy, try not to transfer the juice along with the tomatoes. This can make the dip mushy. Next, sprinkle the olives evenly over the tomatoes, using as much or as little as you like. Finally, sprinkle the sliced scallions over the top of the casserole and serve.

Tip: If you're using a high-speed blender, you can skip the soaking step for the cashews and just use them dry. Add a little extra water to blend if needed.

Variation: If you want to make this recipe nut-free, simply omit the cashews and add a tablespoon of a light-flavored oil (like canola or a light olive oil) for richness.

Loaded Nacho Fries

This casserole was one that my son and I came up with together. He wanted poutine, which is fries topped with cheese and gravy, and I wanted nachos. We compromised and came up with this loaded nacho fries casserole, which left us both fabulously full and happy.

Serves 4 as an appetizer

1 (24-ounce) bag frozen French fries

1 recipe Nacho Cheesy Sauce, thinned slightly to a
    pourable consistency and kept hot (page 176)

1 (15-ounce) can black beans, drained and rinsed

1 large tomato, diced

Chopped fresh cilantro

Sliced scallions

Black olives, pitted and sliced (optional)

Pickled jalapeños (optional)

Preheat the oven to 450°F. Line a large baking sheet with lightly greased parchment paper.

Scatter the frozen fries in an even layer on the prepared baking sheet. Roast in the oven, moving them around as necessary so they evenly brown, until the fries are crispy, for 45 to 50 minutes.

Remove the fries from the oven and place in a 13 x 9-inch baking dish. Top with the prepared cheese sauce, black beans, diced tomato, cilantro, scallions, black olives, and jalapeños, if using. Serve right away.

Gluten-Free: Use gluten-free frozen fries.

Welsh Rarebit Casserole

Welsh rarebit has always been a special dish for my daughter, as it was something that she and her granny Marilyn would order at Dupar's Restaurant. My daughter has asked me for years to come up with a vegan version. This is my modern spin on Welsh rarebit, turning it more into a fondue casserole.

Serves 4 as an appetizer

1 recipe Pub-Style Cream Sauce (page 177)
½ baguette or loaf of French bread, cut
    into ½- to ¾-inch cubes (about 3½ to 4 cups
    of lightly packed bread), lightly toasted
    if desired
Chipotle powder or smoked or regular paprika
    (optional)
Freshly ground black pepper to taste

Preheat the oven to 400°F. Grease an 8-inch square glass or ceramic baking dish.

Prepare the sauce. Place half the bread cubes in the prepared baking dish. Top with half the sauce. Layer the remaining bread cubes over the sauce and top with the remaining sauce. If desired, sprinkle the top with a dusting of chipotle powder. Bake for 15 to 20 minutes, or until bubbly and hot. Remove from the oven, add black pepper to taste, and serve.

Gluten-Free: Use gluten-free bread, as well as a gluten-free oat flour in the Pub-Style Cream Sauce.

Chapter Two

Dutch-Oven and Skillet Casseroles

Aloo Gobi

This recipe is slightly adapted from a recipe by cookbook author Anupy Singla. I have always adored aloo gobi, and this version is pure deliciousness. It's a one-pot wonder, with fragrantly spiced cauliflower, onions, tomatoes, and potatoes.

Serves 4

1 to 2 tablespoons canola oil

2 teaspoons cumin seeds

1 teaspoon ground turmeric

1 large yellow or red onion, diced

1 teaspoon plus pinch of fine sea salt, divided

2 heaping tablespoons grated or minced fresh ginger

4 cloves garlic, minced or pressed

1 medium to large potato, peeled and diced

1 jalapeño, finely sliced (optional)

1 medium head cauliflower, trimmed and cut into small florets

2 teaspoons garam masala

1 teaspoon ground coriander

1 cup undrained canned diced tomatoes, preferably organic

¼ cup hot water, plus more as needed

1 heaping tablespoon minced fresh cilantro

In a Dutch oven or 4-quart sauté pan with a lid, heat the oil over medium-high heat. Once warm, add the cumin and turmeric. Cook until the seeds sizzle and turn reddish-brown, about 40 seconds.

Add the onion and pinch of salt. Cook for 2 to 4 minutes, until the onions brown slightly, stirring occasionally. Add the ginger and garlic. Cook for another 40 seconds, stirring occasionally. Add the potato and jalapeño, if using, and cook for 1 to 2 minutes, until the potato softens slightly. Add the cauliflower, garam masala, coriander, and 1 teaspoon salt. Mix well until all the florets are yellow from the turmeric. Cook for about 2 minutes and then add the tomatoes and water.

Cover the pan, turn the heat down to medium-low, and cook for 20 to 25 minutes, or until the vegetables are soft, stirring occasionally. Cook a little less if you want a tiny bit of crunch, and cook a little longer if you want the vegetables to be a little softer. Add up to ½ cup additional water if the vegetable mixture is too thick.

Remove from the heat, add the cilantro, and put the lid back on. Let the aloo gobi sit for 3 to 5 minutes before serving to help the flavors all come together. Serve with roti, naan, or basmati rice.

Skillet Chilaquiles

This is my take on chilaquiles, and it is just as fantastic for breakfast as it is for dinner. It takes the humble tofu scramble to an all-time high, with the addition of corn tortillas, peppers, onions, and savory home-made enchilada sauce. If you like to spice things up, add a little chipotle powder or hot sauce too.

Serves 3 to 4

1 tablespoon olive oil
½ cup diced yellow onion, plus more for garnish
2 cloves garlic, pressed or minced
¼ green bell pepper, diced
14 ounces extra firm tofu, drained
1 cup frozen corn, thawed
1½ teaspoons granulated onion
½ teaspoon granulated garlic
½ teaspoon sea salt
¼ teaspoon ground cumin
4 corn tortillas, torn into pieces
1 recipe Everyday Enchilada Sauce (page 183)
Tortilla chips
1 medium Roma tomato, diced, for garnish
Chopped fresh cilantro, for garnish
Diced avocado, for garnish (optional)

Preheat the broiler to high.

Heat the oil in a 10-inch cast-iron skillet over medium-high heat. Add ½ cup of the onion, the garlic, and the pepper and cook, stirring often, until the vegetables start to brown, for about 5 minutes. Crumble the tofu into the skillet, stirring well. Cook the tofu for 5 minutes, stirring as needed. Add the corn, granulated onion, granulated garlic, salt, and cumin. Cook for about 5 minutes, stirring as needed, or until the vegetables are softened.

Add the corn tortillas to the skillet, stirring to mix them in. Stir in 1 cup of the enchilada sauce and continue cooking. The tortillas should start absorbing the sauce, and the mixture should become a little drier. Stir in another ½ cup of the enchilada sauce and let cook for another minute or two, stirring as necessary. Crush a handful of tortilla chips over the top and carefully place the skillet under the broiler. Broil for about 5 minutes, or until the mixture starts to puff up a little and the chips on top start to get a little brown and toasty. Remove from the oven.

If the scramble looks dry, drizzle additional enchilada sauce over the top. Sprinkle the top of the scramble with another handful of crushed tortilla chips, diced onion, diced tomatoes, chopped cilantro, and avocado, if using. Serve the chilaquiles hot, with the remaining enchilada sauce on the side.

Pale Ale Stew

Who would have thought that a stew could be so easy to make, yet taste like it's been cooking for hours? I owe a nod to my brother Jon for suggesting this recipe, which has now become a favorite wintertime dish. Make sure to prepare the gravy in a larger-than-necessary pot or Dutch oven so that you have plenty of room to add the stew.

Serves 6

1 pound small Yukon gold or red-skinned
  potatoes (about 4 to 7), rinsed and cubed
1 recipe Savory Gravy (page 171),
  made with the pale ale variation
6 ounces sliced or halved button or cremini
  mushrooms
8 ounces frozen pearl onions
6 ounces (about 3 cups) broccoli or
  cauliflower florets
1½ cups frozen peas
Salt and freshly ground black pepper to taste

In a medium saucepan, add the potatoes and cover with water. Place over high heat and bring to a boil. Boil for 10 to 15 minutes, or until the potatoes are just fork-tender. Drain and set aside.

Heat the gravy in a large pot or Dutch oven. Add the mushrooms and onions. Simmer for about 10 minutes, or until the mushrooms are tender. Add the potatoes and broccoli and cook for about 5 minutes, or until the broccoli is just tender and bright green. Stir in the frozen peas, and cook for 1 more minute. Add salt and pepper to taste and serve.

Tip: This stew is fantastic served over mashed potatoes or cooked polenta. You can also swap the vegetables out for others, depending on what you have in your fridge or which vegetables are in season.

Gluten-Free: Use a gluten-free beer, as well as a gluten-free oat flour, in the gravy recipe.

Jambalaya

Jambalaya is the perfect one-pot meal, with spicy flavors and lots of fresh vegetables. I love to make this dish when we go camping, or whenever I have a big group over for dinner. Although you might be tempted to substitute brown rice for the white, this dish comes out best with long-grain white rice.

Serves 6

1 tablespoon olive oil

1 large yellow onion, sliced into ¼-inch crescents

4 cloves garlic, smashed, pressed, or minced

2 green bell peppers, chopped

4 ribs celery, cut into ¼-inch slices

1¼ cups uncooked long-grain white rice, unrinsed

1½ cups drained canned diced tomatoes, preferably organic

2 cups vegetable broth, or 2 cups hot water with a vegan vegetable bouillon cube or powder to taste (the Cajun seasoning is also very salty on its own)

1 to 3 tablespoons Cajun or Creole seasoning (with salt added)

1½ teaspoons smoked paprika

Salt and freshly ground black pepper to taste

Heat the oil in a large Dutch oven or heavy pot with a lid over medium-high heat. Add the onion, garlic, peppers, and celery and sauté for several minutes until slightly softened. Add the rice and sauté for 1 minute more. Add the tomatoes, broth, Cajun seasoning, and paprika and stir well.

Bring the mixture to a boil, reduce the heat to medium-low, cover, and simmer for about 30 minutes, or until the rice is tender and most of the liquid has been absorbed. (You may need to reduce the heat to low if your stove runs hot and the rice starts to stick.)

Remove the pot from the heat and let sit, covered, for 10 minutes. Add salt and pepper to taste and serve the jambalaya hot.

Tip: Use a 28-ounce can of diced tomatoes for this recipe and measure once you've drained out all of the liquid. For the seasoning, I really like Tony Chachere's Original Creole Seasoning in this recipe. I usually add 2 to 3 tablespoons (rather than 1), but it gives it a big kick, so be sure to add it to taste.

Variation: If desired, add sliced vegan sausages, sliced seitan, or vegan chicken or cooked Soy Curls to the jambalaya.

Gluten-Free: Use gluten-free bouillon and Cajun seasoning.

Moroccan Vegetable Stew

I fell in love with this dish on a trip to London years ago. Many of the restaurants that we went to offered this dish as a vegan alternative, which brought a giant smile to my face. The stew was brimming with the most incredibly fragrant, sweet flavors of cinnamon, turnips, sweet potatoes, and saffron.

Serves 4 to 6

1 to 2 tablespoons olive oil

1 small yellow onion, diced

4 to 6 cloves garlic, finely minced or pressed

2 small carrots, cut into ¼-inch coins

2 small sweet potatoes, peeled and cut into ½-inch pieces

2 large turnips, peeled and cut into ½-inch pieces

2 teaspoons ground cumin

2 teaspoons granulated sugar or agave

1 teaspoon ground cinnamon

¼ teaspoon ground allspice

1 (15-ounce) can diced tomatoes, preferably organic, undrained

3½ cups vegetable broth, or 3½ cups hot water mixed with a vegan vegetable bouillon cube or powder to taste

2 medium zucchini, sliced in half lengthwise, then sliced into ½-inch pieces

1 (15-ounce) can chickpeas, drained and rinsed (1½ cups)

2 pinches saffron threads

Salt and freshly ground black pepper to taste

2¼ cups water

1½ cups uncooked quinoa, rinsed and drained in a fine sieve

⅓ cup golden raisins

Chopped fresh cilantro, for garnish

(recipe continues)

In a large Dutch oven or high-sided skillet, heat the oil over medium-high heat. Add the onion and cook, stirring as needed, for 5 minutes, or until the onions are starting to soften. Add the garlic and cook for another 5 minutes, or until the onions are starting to become golden. Add the carrots, sweet potatoes, and turnips and stir well. Sprinkle the cumin, sugar, cinnamon, and allspice over the vegetables, giving them a good stir to coat. Add the diced tomatoes and cook, stirring occasionally, until the sweet potatoes and turnips are beginning to soften, for 5 to 10 minutes. Stir in the broth, zucchini, and chickpeas. Bring the mixture to a boil. Crumble the saffron threads into the mixture. Reduce the heat to a simmer and partially cover. Continue cooking for 20 minutes, or until the vegetables are soft and tender and the stew is thick. Add salt and pepper to taste.

While the stew is cooking, prepare the quinoa. In a medium saucepan, combine the hot water and the quinoa and bring to a simmer. Add the golden raisins, give it a quick stir, cover, and reduce the heat to low. Let the quinoa cook for 15 minutes. Remove the pot from the heat. Leave the pot covered and set aside until the stew is done.

Serve the hot stew over the cooked quinoa and sprinkle the top with chopped cilantro.

Campfire Chili

This recipe was inspired by Bryanna Clark Grogan's award-winning chili recipe. It works really well in the casserole recipes that call for chili, or just served out of the pot alongside some toasty cornbread. It comes together super-quick and tastes like it simmered for hours. It's my favorite campfire meal.

Serves 4 hungry campers

1 tablespoon olive oil

½ yellow onion, chopped

3 cloves garlic, minced or pressed

1 bell pepper, any color, finely chopped

3 cups hot water

2 (15-ounce) cans kidney beans, drained and rinsed

1 (6-ounce) can tomato paste

3 tablespoons tamari or soy sauce

2 tablespoons Homemade Chili Powder (page 175), or 2 tablespoons plus 2 teaspoons store-bought chili powder, or to taste

1 tablespoon cocoa powder

2 teaspoons granulated onion

1½ teaspoons ground cumin

1½ teaspoons dried oregano

1 teaspoon fine sea salt

¾ cup TSP or TVP granules, preferably organic

Ground chipotle powder (optional)

In a large saucepan, add the oil and heat over medium-high heat. Add the onion and garlic and cook, stirring occasionally, until the onions are starting to soften and turn golden, for 5 to 6 minutes. Add the bell pepper and cook, stirring, for another 3 minutes.

Add the hot water and the beans, tomato paste, tamari, chili powder, cocoa, granulated onion, cumin, oregano, and salt, stirring well. Bring the mixture to a simmer. Stir in the TSP and reduce the heat to low. If you're using the ground chipotle powder, add it now.

Let the chili simmer over low heat, partially covered, for 15 minutes. Adjust the seasonings to taste and serve.

Gluten-Free: Use gluten-free tamari or soy sauce.

Veggies and Dumplings

This recipe is from my book *Vegan Diner*, and it practically has its own fan club. It's an old-fashioned favorite that tastes just like Grandma's dumplings, had Grandma been vegan. There's nothing quite like a warm bowl of this hearty stew in the winter to keep you warm. It can easily be made in under an hour.

Serves 4 to 6

STEW

6 cups hot water

2 to 3 tablespoons vegan chicken broth powder or base, or more to taste

3 tablespoons nutritional yeast flakes

2 teaspoons granulated onion or onion powder

4 large carrots, cut into ¼-inch coins

4 ribs celery, cut into ¼-inch coins

1 small yellow or white onion, finely diced

½ cup plain unsweetened soymilk

½ cup unbleached all-purpose flour

1 tablespoon dried parsley flakes or 3 tablespoons minced fresh parsley

1 teaspoon fine sea salt, or more to taste

Freshly ground black pepper to taste

2 cups coarsely chopped broccoli

1 cup frozen peas

Dried or minced fresh dill, for garnish (optional)

DUMPLINGS

2 cups unbleached all-purpose flour

1 tablespoon baking powder

½ teaspoon fine sea salt

2 tablespoons canola oil

¾ cup plus 2 tablespoons plain unsweetened soymilk or other nondairy milk

FOR THE STEW

In a large pot or Dutch oven, combine the hot water with the broth powder, nutritional yeast, granulated onion, carrots, celery, and onion. Bring to a simmer over medium-high heat. Reduce the heat to maintain a slow simmer, partially cover, and cook for 20 minutes, or until vegetables are just tender.

Using an immersion blender or regular blender, combine the soymilk, flour, and ½ cup of water. Blend until smooth. Slowly whisk the flour mixture into the broth and vegetables. Continue whisking until the soup is thickened. Whisk in the parsley. Add 1 teaspoon of salt and the pepper to taste. Whisking continuously, bring to a simmer. Stir the broccoli and peas into the soup.

FOR THE DUMPLINGS

In a medium bowl, combine the flour, baking powder, and salt, mixing well. Add the oil and soymilk, stirring until the dough is moistened and just comes together. Do not overmix.

Drop the dumpling dough by small spoonfuls, one at a time, into the thickened stew. Cover the pot, reduce the heat, and simmer for 15 minutes. Make sure not to peek by removing the lid, as the dumplings need to steam. After 15 minutes, uncover the pot and check to make sure that the dumplings are cooked through. If not, cover the pot and simmer for another 5 minutes. Sprinkle dill over the top, if desired, and ladle the stew and dumplings into bowls. Serve right away.

Variation: Reconstitute 1 cup dried Soy Curls in ¾ cup hot water. Drain well, squeezing the extra water from them. Coarsely chop them and stir into the stew along with the broccoli.

Baby Greens with Cashew Cream Sauce

One of my favorite dishes growing up was creamed spinach. I haven't had the dairy version in years, but this is a perfect re-creation, with a combination of baby kale, chard, and spinach, bathed in a creamy cashew sauce. I adapted the original recipe from Whole Foods Market. Feel free to substitute chopped kale for the baby greens blend.

Serves 2 to 4 as a side

1 cup plain unsweetened soymilk or other
   nondairy milk

¼ cup raw unsalted cashews, soaked for at
   least 2 hours and drained

2 tablespoons nutritional yeast flakes

1 teaspoon granulated onion

1 tablespoon white miso paste

2 teaspoons olive oil

1 large shallot, finely minced

2 cloves garlic, pressed or minced

6 cups mixed baby greens (such as kale, chard,
   and spinach) or chopped kale or other
   dark, leafy green

In a blender, combine the soymilk, cashews, nutritional yeast, granulated onion, and miso and purée until smooth and silky.

Heat the oil in a large, nonreactive skillet over medium-high heat. Add the shallot and garlic and cook until they just turn golden. Add the cashew cream mixture to the skillet and bring to a simmer. Stir in the greens, folding them into the sauce until they begin to wilt. Continue to simmer, stirring often, until the greens are tender, for about 5 minutes. If the sauce is too thick, you can thin it with a little bit of water.

Tip: If you're using a high-speed blender, you can skip the soaking step for the cashews and just use them dry. Add a little extra water to blend if needed.

Rustic White Beans with Sage and Garlic

This delicious dish with white beans, tomatoes, and sage reminds me of the French bean dish *cassoulet*, albeit without the meat. When I was growing up, my mother made the best cassoulet, which was the ultimate in comfort food. This is my vegan nod to my mother's special dish.

Serves 4 to 6

2 cups dried Great Northern beans, soaked overnight, rinsed, and drained

4 cups hot water, plus more as needed

1 bay leaf

1 sprig fresh rosemary

1 (15-ounce) can diced tomatoes, preferably organic, undrained and coarsely puréed

2 tablespoons nutritional yeast flakes

2 teaspoons granulated onion

1 teaspoon smoked paprika

¾ teaspoon dried sage

2 vegan bouillon cubes, preferably mushroom

4 cloves garlic, minced or pressed

Salt and freshly ground black pepper to taste

¼ cup minced fresh parsley

2 recipes Buttery Crumb Topping (page 162)

In a large Dutch oven, combine the soaked beans, hot water, bay leaf, and rosemary. Bring the beans to a boil, reduce the heat to a low simmer, partially cover, and cook for 1 hour, or until the beans are very tender. Check the beans periodically to give a little stir and make sure that the water doesn't cook out. Add a little more water as needed, up to ½ cup. You don't want to drown the beans in water, however, as this should be a fairly thick stew.

Once the beans are tender, add the tomatoes, nutritional yeast, granulated onion, paprika, sage, bouillon cubes, and garlic to the pot. Add salt and pepper to taste. Stir in the parsley. Let the beans simmer for about 15 minutes. This will give the beans a chance to thicken up into a stew and allow time for the flavors to meld. Remove the rosemary sprig and bay leaf. Preheat the broiler to high while you make the topping.

Sprinkle the prepared crumb topping evenly over the beans.

Carefully transfer the pot of beans to the oven. Broil just until the crumb topping is golden brown. Remove from the oven and serve.

Tip: My favorite mushroom bouillon cubes are made by Knorr; the porcini-flavored bouillon is made in Italy and can be found in Italian markets or online. You can use dried navy beans if you can't find Great Northern.

Gluten-Free: Use gluten-free breadcrumbs in the crumb topping recipe and gluten-free bouillon cubes. My favorite brand of store-bought gluten-free breadcrumbs is Ian's Panko-style.

Chapter Three

◆◆◆

Old Favorites
and New Twists

Very Veggie Pot Pie

If my family were stranded on a desert island and could bring one thing with them, I have a hunch that they would choose this pot pie. It's become our Thanksgiving tradition, but we love it anytime of the year. You can top it with puff pastry, pie dough, or even cornbread.

Serves 4 to 6

8 ounces yellow- or red-skinned potatoes (about 2 medium)

2 large carrots, cut into ⅛-inch-thick coins

3 ounces dried Soy Curls (about 2 cups)

1 cup boiling water

1 tablespoon tamari

1 teaspoon liquid smoke (optional)

3 cups fresh broccoli florets

1 cup frozen peas

1 recipe Savory Gravy (page 171)

Salt and freshly ground black pepper to taste

1 recipe Flaky Pie Dough (page 187), rolled out into a rectangle slightly bigger than your casserole dish

Soymilk or other nondairy milk, for brushing

Preheat the oven to 425°F. Grease a 13 x 9-inch glass or ceramic baking dish.

In a large saucepan, cover the potatoes with an inch or two of water and bring to a boil. Reduce the heat slightly and continue cooking the potatoes at a rapid simmer for about 10 minutes. When the potatoes are almost tender, add the carrots to the pot and continue cooking until the carrots and potatoes are tender, for 5 to 8 minutes. Remove from the heat, drain, and let cool to the touch. Peel the potatoes and cut into pieces.

In a medium bowl, combine the Soy Curls, boiling water, and tamari. Let sit for 10 minutes, or until the Soy Curls are reconstituted. Carefully drain the hot Soy Curls in a colander, pressing out as much liquid as you can. Place the Soy Curls in a large mixing bowl and drizzle the liquid smoke on top, if using, mixing well. Add the potatoes, carrots, broccoli, and peas. Stir in the gravy and add salt and pepper to taste.

(recipe continues)

Scoop the mixture into the prepared baking dish. Place your rolled-out pie dough on top and crimp the edges to seal in the filling. Take a sharp knife and cut four slits in the center of the casserole to let the steam escape. Brush the pastry top with soymilk. Bake for 35 to 45 minutes, or until the pastry top is nicely brown and cooked through.

Tip: If you don't like liquid smoke, feel free to omit it from this recipe.

Variation: Substitute a puff pastry crust for the pie dough. You can also substitute an additional 2 cups of vegetables or seitan for the Soy Curls.

Gluten-Free: Substitute a gluten-free pie dough for the regular pastry. My favorite gluten-free piecrust mix is from Bob's Red Mill. It is so good that no one suspects it's gluten-free.

Smoky Corn and Cheddar Quiche

This casserole is a crowd-pleaser, with smoky Southwestern flavors and a creamy quiche filling. The filling is adapted from a recipe by Clara Iuliano.

Serves 4 as a side dish

1 (14-ounce) box firm tofu (not silken)

¼ cup plain unsweetened soymilk or other nondairy milk, plus up to 4 tablespoons more as needed

½ cup raw unsalted cashews, soaked for at least 2 hours and drained

3 tablespoons nutritional yeast flakes

3 tablespoons cornstarch

1 tablespoon granulated onion

1 teaspoon smoked paprika

¾ to 1 teaspoon salt, or more to taste

2 cloves garlic, minced or pressed

1½ cups frozen sweet corn, thawed and drained

½ cup diced scallions

½ cup shredded vegan Cheddar

Freshly ground black pepper to taste

Preheat the oven to 350°F. Grease an 11 x 7-inch glass or ceramic baking dish.

In a powerful blender, combine the tofu, soymilk, and cashews until smooth. Add the nutritional yeast, cornstarch, granulated onion, paprika, salt, and granulated garlic, blending again until the mixture is ultra-smooth. If your tofu mixture is very thick and not blending well, you can add up to 4 tablespoons additional milk if needed. Only add it if it is necessary to keep the blender moving.

Transfer the blended tofu mixture to a bowl. Stir in the corn, scallions, and cheese. Add salt and pepper to taste. Spread the mixture into the prepared baking dish, smoothing the top. Bake for 35 to 45 minutes, or until the top is firm to the touch and the casserole is baked through. There may be some cracks on the top. Let cool for 15 minutes and serve.

Tip: This casserole is great made ahead of time and refrigerated, which gives the flavors and textures time to meld. You can reheat it in the microwave, or serve it chilled or at room temperature.

If you're using a high-speed blender, you can skip the soaking step for the cashews and just use them dry. Add a little extra water to blend if needed.

Variation: For a bacony twist, stir ⅓ cup Bakin' Bits (page 163) into the quiche mixture before baking.

Olive and Sun-Dried Tomato Quiche with Hash Brown Crust

This would be a perfect casserole to serve at a brunch or to bring to a potluck. It's full of delicious Mediterranean flavors, including olives, sun-dried tomatoes, and basil.

Serves 4 as a side dish

3 cups shredded frozen hash browns, thawed and drained (if necessary), at room temperature

3 tablespoons nonhydrogenated vegan margarine, melted

3 tablespoons nutritional yeast flakes, divided

2 teaspoons granulated garlic or garlic powder, divided

Salt and freshly ground black pepper to taste

1 (14-ounce) box firm tofu (not silken)

¼ cup plain unsweetened soymilk or other nondairy milk, plus up to 4 tablespoons more as needed

½ cup raw unsalted cashews, soaked for at least 2 hours and drained

3 tablespoons cornstarch

3 cloves garlic, minced or pressed

2 teaspoons granulated onion

1 teaspoon dried marjoram

½ teaspoon dried thyme

1 teaspoon fine sea salt

½ cup sliced pitted Kalamata olives

½ cup sun-dried tomatoes, julienned

¼ to ½ cup shredded vegan mozzarella (optional)

Preheat the oven to 450°F. Grease an 11 x 7-inch glass or ceramic baking dish.

If your thawed hash browns feel at all soggy, gently press them between paper towels to blot them as dry as possible. In the prepared baking dish, mix the hash browns with the melted margarine, 1 tablespoon nutritional yeast, 1 teaspoon granulated garlic, and salt and pepper to taste. Press them into the bottom and three-quarters up the sides to form a crust. Bake for 35 to 45 minutes, or until golden brown and starting to crisp. Remove the baking dish from the oven. Reduce the oven temperature to 350°F.

In a powerful blender, combine the tofu, soymilk, cashews, cornstarch, remaining 2 tablespoons nutritional yeast, garlic, granulated onion, marjoram, thyme, sea salt, and remaining 1 teaspoon granulated garlic. Blend until ultra-smooth. If your tofu mixture is very thick and not blending well, you can add up to 4 tablespoons additional milk if needed. Only add it if it is necessary to keep the blender moving.

Transfer the blended tofu mixture into a bowl. Stir in the olives, sun-dried tomatoes, and cheese, if using. Add salt and pepper to taste. Spread the

(recipe continues)

mixture into the baked hash brown crust, smoothing the top. Bake for 35 to 45 minutes, or until the top is firm to the touch and the casserole is baked through. There may be some cracks on the top. Let cool for at least 30 minutes before serving.

Tip: I like to thaw my hash browns in the microwave. Depending on the wattage of your microwave, simply heat in 1-minute intervals until defrosted and warm. The added warmth will also help keep the margarine from hardening when you mix them.

If you're using a high-speed blender, you can skip the soaking step for the cashews and just use them dry. Add a little extra water to blend if needed.

Gluten-Free: Use gluten-free hash browns.

Hash Brown Gratin

Just the mention of a gratin will instantly elicit excitement from casserole lovers. I see it in my kids' eyes. The best part about vegan gratins is that they aren't loaded down with pounds of cheese and butter—just a delicious sauce and lots of flavor.

Serves 4

3 recipes Cream of Vegan Chicken Soup
   (page 167)
½ cup nondairy vegan sour cream
1 (20-ounce) bag frozen hash browns, thawed
Freshly ground black pepper to taste
Finely minced fresh parsley, for garnish

Preheat the oven to 400°F. Grease an 8-inch square glass or ceramic baking dish.

In a large bowl, gently mix the soup, sour cream, and thawed hash browns. Add a few grinds of black pepper and adjust seasonings to taste. Gently mix well until the hash browns are coated. Scoop the potato mixture into the prepared baking dish. Sprinkle the top with the parsley and bake for 30 minutes, or until hot, puffed, and bubbly around the edges. If desired, place the casserole under the broiler for the last couple of minutes to brown the top. Remove from the oven and serve hot.

Tip: To make quick work of defrosting the hash browns, thaw them in the microwave on 1-minute intervals until thawed and warm.

Variation: Substitute a triple batch of Cream of Mushroom Soup (page 168) in place of the Cream of Vegan Chicken. You can also fold in some chopped vegan chicken before baking.

Gluten-Free: Use gluten-free hash browns and a gluten-free oat flour in the soup.

Nacho Tots Casserole

The first time I made this recipe, my daughter and her boyfriend ate the entire pan. My son was so distraught that I had to make him a pan as well. Potato tots are meant to be baked in a creamy nacho sauce. It's just the way it is.

Serves 4

TOT BASE

1 tablespoon olive oil, plus more as needed

1 large yellow onion, diced

½ cup thinly sliced scallions

2 to 4 tablespoons vinegary hot sauce, such as Frank's RedHot (optional)

1 recipe Nacho Cheesy Sauce (page 176)

Fine sea salt and freshly ground black pepper to taste

1 (2-pound) bag frozen potato tots, thawed

Chipotle powder or paprika

OPTIONAL TOPPINGS

1 cup Chicken-Style Soy Curls (page 166)

1 cup pinto or black beans

Chopped tomatoes

Chopped fresh cilantro

Thinly sliced scallions

Preheat the oven to 400°F. Grease a 13 x 9-inch glass baking dish with shortening or olive oil.

In a large cast-iron skillet, heat the oil over medium-high heat. Add the onion and cook, stirring occasionally, for about 15 minutes, or until the onions are softened and lightly browned.

Stir the scallions and hot sauce into the cheese sauce. Add salt and pepper to taste.

In a large bowl, combine the thawed potato tots and the onions. Gently fold the sauce into the tots and onions, just until the tots are coated. Scoop the tot mixture into the prepared baking dish. Sprinkle the top with chipotle powder and bake for 15 minutes. If you are adding the optional toppings, sprinkle with the Chicken-Style Soy Curls and/or the beans. Bake another 5 to 10 minutes, or until the casserole is really hot. Remove from the oven and top with chopped tomatoes, cilantro, and scallions and serve.

Gluten-Free: Use gluten-free potato tots and a gluten-free oat flour in the cheese sauce.

Variation: You can take the loaded toppings another step further by adding dollops of guacamole and corn chips to the baked casserole.

Creamy Rice and Dill Casserole

My daughter requested this casserole for dinner one night, and it quickly became a favorite. It's a creamy, white wine–infused dish with Soy Curls, lots of fresh dill, and rice. Look for a super-flavorful vegan chicken bouillon, such as Better Than Bouillon No Chicken Base, which makes this casserole even better.

Serves 4

2 cups cooked long-grain white or brown rice

2 cups Chicken-Style Soy Curls (page 166), coarsely chopped, or other store-bought vegan chicken

8 ounces frozen spinach, thawed and squeezed dry

1 recipe Almost Alfredo Sauce with white wine variation (page 180)

1 tablespoon vegan chicken base, such as Better Than Bouillon, or more to taste

3 tablespoons minced fresh dill, or 2 teaspoons dried dill

2 tablespoons freshly squeezed lemon juice

2 teaspoons granulated onion

3 cloves garlic, minced or pressed

Salt and freshly ground black pepper to taste

Preheat the oven to 400°F. Grease an 8-inch square glass or ceramic baking dish.

In a large bowl, combine the rice, Soy Curls, spinach, sauce, vegan chicken base, dill, lemon, granulated onion, and garlic, mixing until the rice is coated. Add salt and pepper to taste.

Scoop the mixture into the prepared baking dish. Bake for 20 to 30 minutes, or until hot and puffed. Remove from the oven and serve hot.

Tip: If you have leftover rice, this casserole is a perfect way to use it up.

Variation: You can substitute 2 to 3 cups of cooked quinoa for the rice. You can also substitute diced seitan in place of the Soy Curls or vegan chicken.

Mujadara

I've always had a soft spot in my heart for mujadara, with its sweet flavor of caramelized onions layered with fluffy rice and savory lentils. It is a deliciously comforting dish. This recipe is adapted from a mujadara recipe by Faith Durand, who had the brilliant idea of baking it all together in a casserole dish, without precooking the rice or lentils.

Serves 4 to 6

1 tablespoon olive oil

1 large yellow or sweet onion, cut in half and thinly sliced

½ teaspoon sea salt

¾ cup brown lentils

¾ cup uncooked brown or white basmati rice

1 teaspoon ground cumin

4 cups steaming-hot vegetable broth, or 4 cups steaming-hot water with 1 to 1½ tablespoons vegan chicken base, such as Better Than Bouillon, or to taste

Salt and freshly ground black pepper to taste

Minced fresh parsley, for garnish

Heat the oil in a large cast-iron skillet over medium-high heat. Add the onion and sprinkle with the salt. Cook for 5 minutes, stirring as needed. Reduce the heat to medium and continue cooking, stirring occasionally, for about 25 minutes, or until the onions are a deep brown color.

Meanwhile, preheat the oven to 400°F. Grease a 13 x 9-inch glass or ceramic baking dish.

Scoop the caramelized onions into the prepared baking dish. Stir in the lentils, rice, cumin, and hot vegetable broth. Cover the baking dish tightly with a double layer of aluminum foil and bake for 1 hour, if using white basmati rice, or 75 minutes if using brown basmati rice, until the rice and lentils are tender and have absorbed all of the liquid. Add salt and pepper to taste and sprinkle with minced parsley.

Make It Your Way Casserole

I've come up with a blueprint for making your own casserole. Depending on your mood, or what vegetables and cooked grains you have in your fridge, you can create a delicious casserole all your own. Remember that this is only a blueprint, so you can add whatever combo of spices, veggies, cooked grains, and sauce you like.

Serves 4

Choose one of the following: 2 cups cooked long-grain white or brown rice, 2 cups cooked barley, or 3 cups cooked quinoa

Choose one of the following: 1 recipe Cheesy Sauce (page 178), 1 recipe Almost Alfredo Sauce (page 180), 3 recipes Cream of Vegan Chicken Soup (page 167), or 3 recipes Cream of Mushroom Soup (page 168)

About 2 cups sautéed, lightly steamed, or roasted vegetables of choice

Salt and freshly ground black pepper to taste

Seasonings of choice to taste

Crispy toppings such as cracker crumbs, crushed chips, panko, crushed gluten-free rice cereal, or Buttery Crumb Topping (page 162)

Preheat the oven to 400°F. Grease an 8-inch square glass or ceramic baking dish.

In a large bowl, combine the cooked grains with the prepared sauce or soup and the vegetables, mixing until everything is well coated. Add salt, pepper, and seasonings to taste. Scoop the mixture into the prepared baking dish. Sprinkle the topping over the casserole and bake for 20 to 30 minutes, or until hot. Serve hot.

Tip: You can mix in about a cup or so of cooked beans or diced vegan chicken before baking.

Gluten-Free: Use gluten-free grains, along with a gluten-free sauce and topping.

Bean and Rice Casserole

This has become one of our "go-to" recipes for quick and hearty weeknight meals. It also helps if you make large batches of rice and beans, so that you have most of the ingredients at the ready. This casserole is also really good served with homemade Salsa Fresca (page 182).

Serves 4

1 recipe Nacho Cheesy Sauce (page 176) or
   Cheesy Sauce (page 178)
3 cups cooked and drained pinto beans,
   or canned pinto beans, drained and rinsed
2 cups cooked long-grain white or brown rice
Salt and freshly ground black pepper to taste
Crushed tortilla chips, for garnish
Chopped fresh cilantro, for garnish

Preheat the oven to 400°F. Grease an 8-inch square glass or ceramic baking dish.

In a large bowl, mix together the prepared cheesy sauce, beans, and rice. Add salt and pepper to taste. Scoop the mixture into the prepared baking dish. Bake for 20 to 30 minutes, or until hot, with a nice crust on top. Remove from the oven and top with crushed chips and a sprinkling of cilantro. Serve hot.

Tip: A fun way to serve this casserole is with guacamole, salsa, and tortilla chips on the side.

Hearty Fiesta Rice Casserole

You can never have too many crowd-pleaser casseroles in your back pocket, and this one is no exception. This casserole is a fiesta of rice, Soy Curls, corn, and chiles, tossed with a creamy nacho cheese sauce. Feel free to substitute another vegetarian chicken substitute in place of the Soy Curls.

Serves 4

1 recipe Nacho Cheesy Sauce (page 176)

2 cups cooked long-grain white or brown rice

2 cups Chicken-Style Soy Curls (page 166), coarsely chopped, or other store-bought vegan chicken

1 cup frozen sweet corn, thawed and drained

Small can diced mild green chiles (optional)

Diced jalapeño (optional)

Salt and freshly ground black pepper to taste

Minced fresh cilantro, for garnish

4 to 5 scallions, sliced (about ½ cup), for garnish

Preheat the oven to 400°F. Grease an 8-inch square glass or ceramic baking dish.

In a large bowl, combine the cheese sauce, rice, and Soy Curls, mixing until everything is well coated. Add the corn and diced chiles and jalapeño, if using. Add salt and pepper to taste. Scoop the mixture into the prepared baking dish. Bake for 20 to 30 minutes, or until hot, with a nice crust on top. Remove from the oven, sprinkle with cilantro and scallions, and serve.

Variation: If you like things spicy, you can add extra jalapeño peppers or hot sauce (like Sriracha or a vinegary-style hot sauce like Frank's) to taste. You can also top the casserole with crushed tortilla or corn chips, or serve them on the side.

Rice and Broccoli Casserole

Being a huge fan of anything with broccoli, rice, and cheese sauce, I felt it was high time to give the quintessential "old-school"–style broccoli casserole a makeover. So I went straight to the kitchen and created my modern version, which I dare say is absolutely delicious and so much better than the original.

Serves 4

8 ounces (about 4 cups) fresh broccoli florets
1 recipe Cheesy Sauce (page 178)
2 cups cooked long-grain white or brown rice
2 cups Chicken-Style Soy Curls (page 166), coarsely chopped, or other store-bought vegan chicken
Salt and freshly ground black pepper to taste
Sriracha or other hot sauce (optional)

Preheat the oven to 400°F. Grease an 8-inch square glass or ceramic baking dish.

In a medium pot with a steamer insert, add water just to the level of the bottom of the steamer. Bring the water to a boil. Add the broccoli florets to the steamer, cover the pot, reduce the heat, and steam for 5 minutes, or just until tender. Transfer the broccoli to a cutting board to cool slightly. Coarsely chop the broccoli and place in a large bowl.

To the broccoli, add the cheese sauce, rice, and Soy Curls, mixing until everything is well coated. Add salt and pepper to taste. If desired, add a teaspoon of Sriracha sauce, or to taste. Scoop the mixture into the prepared baking dish. Bake for 20 to 30 minutes, or until hot, with a nice crust on top. Remove from the oven and serve hot.

If desired, serve Sriracha or other hot sauce on the side.

Variation: For a Soy Curl–less version, simply omit the Soy Curls.

You can also substitute an equal amount of cooked quinoa for the rice.

Layered Polenta and Mushrooms

This casserole seems like it would take so much longer to prepare than it actually does. Tubes of polenta are a great staple to keep in the pantry, and the recipe comes together in a snap—perfect for a quick weeknight meal.

Serves 4

2 tablespoons olive oil, divided, plus more
    as needed
8 ounces cremini or button mushrooms, sliced
2 cloves garlic, minced or pressed
Pinch of dried oregano
1 (8-ounce) tube prepared polenta, sliced
    into ¼-inch rounds
1 recipe Quick Tomato Basil Sauce (page 185),
    or 4 cups store-bought sauce
⅔ cup shredded vegan mozzarella (optional)

Variation: You can substitute sautéed spinach for the mushrooms.

Gluten-Free: Use gluten-free polenta.

Preheat the oven to 400°F. Grease an 8-inch square glass or ceramic casserole dish.

In a large cast-iron skillet, heat 1 tablespoon olive oil over medium heat. Add the mushrooms, garlic, and a pinch or two of dried oregano. Cook the mushrooms and garlic, stirring, for 5 to 8 minutes, or until the mushrooms are softened. Transfer to a plate and set aside.

Wipe out the skillet with a paper towel. Add the remaining 1 tablespoon olive oil and heat over high heat. Working in batches, fry the polenta rounds until golden, about 5 minutes per side. Add additional olive oil if necessary to keep the polenta from sticking to the pan.

Cover the bottom of the prepared baking dish with a layer of the tomato sauce. Place half of the polenta rounds in an even layer over the sauce. Sprinkle the mushrooms on top. Sprinkle with half of the cheese, if using. Cover with another layer of sauce. Place the remaining polenta rounds in an even layer over the sauce. Top with a final layer of sauce, completely covering the polenta. Sprinkle with the remaining cheese, if using. Bake for 20 minutes, or until the mozzarella melts and the sauce is bubbly. Let the casserole sit for 5 minutes before serving.

Shepherd's Pie with Lentils and Herbs

Shepherd's pie might just be the quintessential casserole, from its hearty stew-like filling to the creamy mashed potato topping. This dish does take a bit of work and time to put together, but you are rewarded with a delicious, nourishing casserole when you're done. This seems like the perfect dish to make after a day of skiing or playing in the snow, but it truly can be enjoyed anytime of the year.

Serves 6

TOPPING

2½ pounds red potatoes, peeled
¾ cup plain unsweetened soymilk or almond milk
2 tablespoons nonhydrogenated vegan margarine
2 tablespoons nutritional yeast flakes
2 cloves garlic, pressed or minced
1 teaspoon sea salt
Freshly ground white and black pepper to taste

FILLING

1 cup uncooked brown lentils, rinsed
1 tablespoon olive oil
1 large yellow or sweet onion, diced
5 ounces brown button or baby bella mushrooms, sliced
2 carrots, finely diced
4 cloves garlic, minced
8 ounces Brussels sprouts, thinly sliced
2 teaspoons freshly chopped rosemary leaves
½ teaspoon dried thyme or 1 teaspoon fresh
1 cup frozen peas
1 recipe Good Gravy! (page 174), made with the white wine variation
Salt and freshly ground black pepper to taste

(recipe continues)

FOR THE TOPPING

In a large saucepan, place the potatoes and cover with water. Set over high heat, cover, and bring to a boil. Once boiling, uncover, reduce the heat to medium-high, and cook for 15 minutes, or until tender and easily pierced with a fork. Drain the potatoes and return them to the saucepan. Mash the potatoes using a potato masher and add the soymilk, margarine, nutritional yeast, garlic, salt, and peppers. Continue mashing until the potatoes are smooth and silky. Set aside.

FOR THE FILLING

While the potatoes are cooking, in a medium saucepan place the lentils and cover with several inches of hot tap water. Bring to a boil over high heat. Once boiling, reduce the heat slightly to maintain a simmer and cook for about 30 minutes, or until the lentils are tender but not mushy. Drain them well and set aside.

While the lentils and potatoes are cooking, prepare the filling. In a large cast-iron skillet, heat the oil over medium-high heat. Add the onion, mushrooms, carrots, and garlic and cook until the carrots are almost tender, about 5 minutes. Add the Brussels sprouts and continue cooking, stirring as needed, for another 5 minutes, or until just soft and the carrots are tender. Stir in the cooked lentils, rosemary, thyme, frozen peas, and gravy, mixing well without smashing the lentils. Add salt and pepper and adjust the seasonings to taste. If the gravy mixture isn't hot, heat just until hot to the touch.

Meanwhile, preheat the oven to 425°F. Grease a 13 x 9-inch glass or ceramic baking dish.

Scoop the gravy mixture into the prepared baking dish. Top with the mashed potatoes, smoothing with a spatula or the back of a spoon. Make sure to spread the potatoes all the way to the edges to prevent the filling from bubbling up. Bake for 25 minutes, or just until the potatoes begin to brown and the casserole is hot. Serve hot.

Sloppy Joe Cornbread Casserole

Sometimes a recipe comes to me in the middle of the night, as was the case with this one. It's a fun and delicious combination of sloppy joe filling and a cornbread top. It also reheats really well the next day.

Serves 4 to 6

2 cups TSP or TVP granules, preferably organic

About 1½ cups boiling water

1 tablespoon olive oil, plus more as needed

1 large yellow onion, chopped

6 cloves garlic, minced or pressed

10 ounces cremini or brown button mushrooms, sliced

2 (15-ounce) cans tomato sauce

2 tablespoons tamari or soy sauce

½ teaspoon liquid smoke

1 teaspoon ground cumin

1 teaspoon granulated garlic or garlic powder

1 teaspoon granulated onion

½ teaspoon salt

Fine sea salt and freshly ground black pepper to taste

Dash of cayenne pepper

1 recipe Cornbread batter (page 186), regular or gluten-free

Hot sauce, for serving

Preheat the oven to 400°F. Grease a 10-inch cast-iron skillet with 2-inch-high sides.

In a medium bowl, add the TSP and pour the boiling water over it. Cover tightly with a piece of aluminum foil or plastic wrap. Set aside for 10 minutes to reconstitute.

Meanwhile, in a large skillet over medium-high heat, place the oil and swirl to coat the bottom of the pan. Add the onion and garlic and cook for 5 minutes, stirring often, until the onion is starting to gain some color. If the onion is starting to stick, you can add a tablespoon or two of water or another tablespoon of oil. Add the mushrooms and cook for another 10 minutes, or until the mushrooms have softened. Add the reconstituted TSP, tomato sauce, tamari, liquid smoke, cumin, granulated garlic, granulated onion, and ½ teaspoon salt, stirring until well mixed. Add more salt and some black pepper and cayenne to taste. Cook for another 10 minutes, stirring as needed. Adjust seasonings to taste.

Scoop the hot sloppy joe filling into the prepared skillet. Evenly dollop the cornbread batter over

(recipe continues)

the filling, smoothing the top. Bake for 30 minutes, or until the cornbread is lightly browned on top and a tester inserted into the cornbread top comes out clean.

Remove the casserole from the oven and let cool for 10 minutes before serving. Serve the casserole with hot sauce on the side.

Tip: This casserole is also fantastic reheated in the microwave and served the next day. Believe it or not, the microwave actually makes the cornbread more tender.

Gluten-Free: Use the gluten-free Cornbread variation (page 186) and gluten-free tamari.

Thanksgiving Stuffing

This recipe is one that I make every year for Thanksgiving, but it's so good, it deserves to be enjoyed more often than that. This stuffing is full of flavor, with toasted bread cubes, fresh sage, onions, and celery. Try it topped with homemade gravy. If you like your stuffing on the richer side, add the optional margarine. For best flavor, look for a very flavorful bouillon like Better Than Bouillon No Chicken Base.

Serves 6

1½ cups very hot water

1 to 2 tablespoons vegan chicken bouillon (powder or paste)

7 cups lightly packed cubed French bread (from 1 baguette) or regular soft bread

1 tablespoon olive oil

4 small ribs celery, thinly sliced or chopped

1 small yellow onion, finely chopped

½ cup dried cranberries

2 tablespoons nutritional yeast flakes

2 teaspoons minced fresh sage leaves or 1 teaspoon dried rubbed sage

½ teaspoon dried marjoram

Salt and freshly ground white and black pepper to taste

2 tablespoons nonhydrogenated vegan margarine, melted (optional)

Preheat the oven to 375°F. Lightly grease a 2-quart casserole dish.

In a measuring cup, mix together the hot water and bouillon. In a large bowl, combine the bread cubes and hot broth mixture, tossing until the bread cubes are well coated. Set aside.

In a large skillet over medium-high heat, place the oil and swirl to coat the bottom of the pan. Add the celery and onion and cook, stirring as needed, until tender, for 10 to 15 minutes. If the onion mixture is starting to stick and burn, add a couple tablespoons of water as needed.

Add the sautéed onion mixture to the bread cubes, along with the dried cranberries, nutritional yeast, sage, and marjoram. Add the white and black pepper to taste. Adjust seasonings, adding salt to taste if necessary.

Transfer the mixture to the prepared casserole dish, cover with a lid or foil, and bake for 15 minutes. Uncover, drizzle with the melted margarine, if using, and return to the oven, uncovered. Bake for an additional 35 to 45 minutes, or until lightly browned and crispy on top. Serve hot.

(recipe continues)

Variation: You can also mix in 1 peeled, cored, and diced apple, 1 cup sliced and sautéed mushrooms, or about 1 cup toasted coarsely chopped hazelnuts or pecans before baking.

Gluten-Free: Substitute gluten-free bread or lightly toasted or stale cubes of gluten-free Cornbread (page 186) for the French bread.

Taco Casserole

I love when people have a specific meal for different nights of the week. I was never organized enough to plan out my meals every week and wound up with lots of nights of "We're having pie for dinner because I'm writing a pie book," but it always looked like fun. So why don't we all start a new trend with Taco Casserole Tuesdays? The filling in this casserole is almost a hybrid of taco and burrito.

Serves 4

2 cups TSP or TVP granules, preferably organic

1½ cups boiling water

1 tablespoon olive oil, plus more as needed

1 small yellow onion, diced

2 tablespoons chili powder, preferably homemade (page 175)

1 tablespoon plus 1 teaspoon granulated onion

3 to 4 cloves garlic, minced

½ teaspoon fine sea salt, or more to taste

¼ teaspoon ground chipotle powder, or more to taste (optional)

1 (16-ounce) can vegetarian refried beans

2 large tomatoes, chopped, divided

Freshly ground black pepper to taste

2 cups coarsely broken tortilla chips, plus more as needed

4 to 5 scallions, sliced (about ½ cup), for garnish

¼ to ½ cup shredded vegan Cheddar or Cheesy Sauce (page 178) (optional)

3 cups shredded romaine lettuce, for garnish

Hot sauce, for serving

(recipe continues)

Preheat the oven to 400°F. Grease an 8-inch square glass or ceramic baking dish.

In a small bowl, combine the TSP and boiling water. Cover tightly with plastic wrap or foil and set aside for 10 minutes to reconstitute.

Heat the oil in a large cast-iron skillet over medium-high heat. Add the onion and cook, stir-ring as needed, for 5 minutes, or until softened. Add the reconstituted TSP, along with the chili powder, granulated onion, garlic, salt, and chipo-tle powder, if using, to the skillet. Cook for another 5 minutes or so, until the onion is lightly browned. Stir in the beans and half of the tomatoes, cook-ing until the mixture is hot. Add salt and pepper, if desired, and adjust seasonings to taste.

In the prepared baking dish, place a layer of broken tortilla chips. Top with the bean mixture. Sprinkle with the scallions and the cheese, if using.

Bake for 20 to 25 minutes, or until hot. Top with shredded lettuce and the remaining tomatoes and chips. Serve right away, with hot sauce on the side.

Variation: For a spicy version, sprinkle minced fresh or sliced pickled jalapeños over the baked casserole. One of my testers served her baked casserole with a drizzle of vegan ranch dressing over the top. The variations are endless.

Old-Fashioned Tamale Pie

A casserole book wouldn't be complete without a recipe for an old-fashioned tamale pie. You can top the recipe with either the gluten-free or regular cornbread topping. It's quickest to prepare the cornbread batter while the chili cooks.

Serves 4

1 recipe Campfire Chili (page 45)
1 recipe Cornbread batter (page 186), regular or
    gluten-free

Preheat the oven to 400°F. Grease an 8-inch square glass or ceramic baking dish.

Scoop the prepared chili into the prepared baking dish. Evenly dollop and spread the batter over the top. Bake for 30 minutes, or until the cornbread is baked through and the top is golden.

Gluten-Free: Use the gluten-free Cornbread variation (page 186).

Chapter Four

• • •

Pasta Casseroles

Zucchini Basil Lasagna

Lasagna always sounds like a super-rich and labor-intensive meal. But it doesn't have to be, and even with just a few ingredients, you've got a healthy and delicious dinner. Plus, zucchini and basil are a perfect pair.

Serves 4 to 6

1 (14-ounce) box firm tofu, drained and
    rinsed well
1 cup thinly sliced fresh basil leaves, plus more
    for garnish
⅓ cup nutritional yeast flakes
2 large cloves garlic, minced or pressed
1 teaspoon salt, or more to taste
3½ cups Quick Tomato Basil Sauce (page 185)
    or store-bought tomato sauce
1 (10-ounce) box dried egg-free
    lasagna noodles
1 medium zucchini, shredded on a box grater

Preheat the oven to 400°F. Lightly grease an 8-inch square glass or ceramic baking dish.

In the bowl of a food processor, combine the tofu, basil, nutritional yeast, garlic, and salt. Process until smooth. Adjust seasonings to taste.

In the prepared baking dish, spread an even layer of tomato sauce, just enough to cover the bottom of the dish. Top with an even layer of the dried noodles, breaking and piecing them together as needed. You will probably need about three per layer, depending on your noodles. Top with half of the tofu mixture. Sprinkle half of the zucchini over the tofu. Top with another layer of sauce, about ¾ cup. Top with another layer of noodles, then the remaining tofu mixture and zucchini. Cover with most of the remaining sauce, or as much as needed to completely cover the zucchini. Cover the baking dish tightly with foil and bake for 60 to 70 minutes, or until the noodles are tender when pierced with a knife.

Remove the lasagna from the oven and let sit for 10 minutes. If the lasagna seems a little dry, top with more sauce. Sprinkle thinly sliced basil on top of the lasagna and serve hot.

Gluten-Free: Use a gluten-free no-cook rice pasta like DeBoles brand, or other gluten-free lasagna noodles.

Baked Tomato Garlic Pasta

This is a delicious garlicky pasta that my husband, Jay, has been making for years. When I first went gluten-free, I thought I wouldn't be able to partake anymore. Then I discovered that, in addition to gluten-free pasta, you can also buy gluten-free panko breadcrumbs. Now when I make this casserole, it is every bit as scrumptious as the original recipe, and no one would ever guess that it's gluten-free.

Serves 4 to 6

8 ounces dried spaghetti

2⅔ cups Quick Tomato Basil Sauce (page 185) or store-bought sauce (26 ounces)

1 cup panko breadcrumbs, divided

4 to 6 large cloves garlic, or to taste, pressed or finely minced

8 to 12 large fresh basil leaves, or to taste, thinly sliced

1 to 2 tablespoons olive oil, or as needed

Preheat the oven to 400°F. Grease an 8-inch square glass or ceramic baking dish.

In a large pot of lightly salted boiling water, add the pasta and cook according to package directions until tender. Don't overcook the pasta, especially if you're using one that is gluten-free. Drain the pasta well.

In a large bowl, combine the pasta, sauce, ¾ cup breadcrumbs, garlic, basil, and olive oil. Transfer the pasta mixture into the prepared baking dish. Cover with foil and bake for 15 minutes. Uncover the casserole and sprinkle the remaining ¼ cup breadcrumbs over the top. Continue baking the casserole uncovered for an additional 10 minutes or so, or until the crumbs are lightly browned and the casserole is hot all the way through.

Tip: If you like your pasta saucier, add an additional ½ cup or so of sauce.

Gluten-Free: Use gluten-free spaghetti and gluten-free panko breadcrumbs.

Boozy Baked Penne with Caramelized Onions

Sometimes a casserole comes together in an unexpected way. I made an extra batch of Pub-Style Cream Sauce (page 177), and, instead of mixing it with bread cubes for the Welsh Rarebit Casserole (page 33), I became inspired and tossed it with penne pasta and caramelized onions. It was delish and instantly became a favorite around our house.

Serves 4

1 tablespoon olive oil, plus more as needed

1 jumbo or large sweet onion, cut into quarters and thinly sliced

Pinch of granulated sugar

Fine sea salt to taste

8 ounces dried penne

1 recipe Pub-Style Cream Sauce (page 177)

1 to 2 tablespoons Dijon mustard, depending on how mustardy you like it

½ teaspoon freshly grated nutmeg

Freshly ground white and black pepper to taste

Buttery Crumb Topping (page 162)

Gluten-Free: Use a gluten-free penne, as well as a gluten-free oat flour and beer in the sauce. My favorite gluten-free pasta for this recipe is brown rice penne.

Preheat the oven to 400°F. Grease an 8-inch square glass or ceramic baking dish.

In a large cast-iron skillet, heat the oil over medium-high heat. Add the onions and cook for 5 to 10 minutes or until they are starting to soften and turn golden. Reduce the heat to medium and sprinkle with a pinch of sugar and salt. Continue cooking for another 10 minutes or so, until the onions are soft and nicely browned. Set aside.

While the onions are cooking, boil the pasta. In a large pot of lightly salted boiling water, add the pasta and cook according to package directions until al dente. Don't overcook the pasta, especially if you're using one that is gluten-free. Drain the pasta well and transfer to a large bowl.

To the pasta, add the prepared cream sauce and caramelized onions, mixing until the pasta is thickly coated. Add the Dijon mustard and nutmeg, stirring well. It will seem like a lot of sauce, but the dish really needs all of it. Add salt and white and black pepper to taste. Scoop the pasta mixture into the prepared baking dish and sprinkle the crumb topping over the top. Bake for 20 minutes, or until hot and lightly browned on top. Serve the casserole warm.

Chili Mac Casserole

This dish could also be called Frito Pie Casserole, because it is exactly that. Macaroni tossed with cheese sauce and chili and topped with crushed corn chips and scallions. Pure heaven!

Serves 4

8 ounces dried macaroni

1 recipe Cheesy Sauce (page 178)

2 to 3 cups Campfire Chili (page 45) or store-bought chili, or to taste

Salt and freshly ground black pepper to taste

½ cup packed, thinly sliced scallions (about 4 scallions)

1 cup crushed corn or tortilla chips (such as Fritos)

Preheat the oven to 400°F. Grease an 8-inch square glass or ceramic baking dish.

In a large pot of lightly salted boiling water, add the macaroni and cook according to package directions until tender. Don't overcook the pasta, especially if you're using one that is gluten-free. Drain the pasta well and transfer to a large bowl.

Mix the cheesy sauce and chili with the macaroni, stirring until the pasta is coated. Add salt and pepper to taste and scoop the macaroni into the prepared baking dish. Bake for 25 to 30 minutes, or until the casserole is hot. Remove from the oven and sprinkle scallions and crushed chips over the top. Serve right away.

Tip: Use a gluten-free macaroni, as well as a gluten-free oat flour in the sauce. My favorite gluten-free pasta for this recipe is brown rice macaroni. It's also very good with quinoa macaroni.

Mac and Cheese Casserole

Vegan mac and cheese is one of my favorite casseroles. It's rich and creamy and every bit as toothsome as a conventional mac and cheese, just made in a healthier, guilt-free way.

Serves 4

8 ounces dried macaroni

1 recipe Cheesy Sauce (page 178)

Salt and freshly ground black pepper to taste

¼ teaspoon freshly grated nutmeg
   (optional)

Preheat the oven to 400°F. Grease an 8-inch square glass or ceramic baking dish.

In a large pot of lightly salted boiling water, add the macaroni and cook according to package directions until tender. Don't overcook the pasta, especially if you're using one that is gluten-free. Drain the pasta well and transfer to a large bowl.

Add the prepared sauce to the cooked macaroni, mixing until the pasta is coated. Add salt and pepper to taste. If desired, add the nutmeg. Scoop the macaroni into the prepared baking dish. Bake for 20 to 30 minutes, or until the top is nicely browned and the casserole is heated through. Remove from the oven and serve.

Variation: If desired, for a cheesier casserole, sprinkle the casserole with shredded vegan Cheddar before baking.

Gluten-Free: Use a gluten-free macaroni, as well as a gluten-free oat flour in the sauce. My favorite gluten-free pasta for this recipe is brown rice macaroni. It's also very good with quinoa macaroni.

Mac and Gravy Casserole

This casserole has a lovely savory, stew-like flavor and is super easy to make. It's a perfect fall dinner: I love to eat it curled up in front of the fire. If you like beer, try it with the boozy beer variation, which takes the gravy to new heights.

Serves 4

1 recipe Good Gravy! (page 174),
    preferably the boozy variation
8 ounces dried macaroni
2 cups small broccoli florets
    (about 3½ ounces)
1 cup frozen peas
Salt and freshly ground black pepper
    to taste
Few handfuls of crushed ruffled potato chips

Preheat the oven to 400°F. Grease an 8-inch square glass or ceramic baking dish.

Let the gravy cool for about 15 minutes to thicken. While it's cooling, cook the pasta.

In a large pot of lightly salted boiling water, add the macaroni and cook according to package directions until tender. When the pasta is about 2 minutes away from being done, add the broccoli. Cook just until the broccoli and pasta are al dente. You want the broccoli to be crisp and bright green. Drain the pasta and broccoli and transfer to a large bowl. Alternatively, you can steam the broccoli separately while the pasta cooks. Don't overcook the pasta, especially if you're using one that is gluten-free.

Add the gravy and frozen peas to the cooked macaroni and broccoli, mixing until the macaroni is thickly coated. Add salt and pepper to taste. It will seem like a lot of gravy, but the dish really needs all of the sauce. Scoop the macaroni into the prepared baking dish and sprinkle with the crushed chips. Bake for 20 minutes, or until hot. Serve the casserole warm.

Variation: This recipe is open to lots of variations. Instead of the broccoli, you can substitute 1 to 2 cups lightly steamed mixed veggies or 1 cup cooked vegan chicken pieces. Simply fold the veggies or vegan chicken in with the gravy and macaroni before baking.

Gluten-Free: Use gluten-free macaroni (my favorite here is brown rice macaroni) and a gluten-free oat flour in the gravy, as well as gluten-free beer, if using the boozy variation.

Nacho Mac Casserole

When my son comes home from college for the weekend, this is one of his favorite dishes. It's comfort food through and through, with lots of zesty flavor from the nacho seasoning and a nice crunch from the chips.

Serves 4 to 6

8 ounces dried macaroni

1 recipe Nacho Cheesy Sauce (page 176)

Salt and freshly ground black pepper to taste

¾ cup thinly sliced scallions (about 4 scallions), divided

Ground chipotle powder

1 to 2 cups crushed corn or tortilla chips (such as Fritos), for garnish

Chopped fresh cilantro, for garnish

Preheat the oven to 400°F. Grease an 8-inch square glass or ceramic baking dish.

In a large pot of lightly salted boiling water, add the macaroni and cook according to package directions until al dente. Don't overcook the pasta, especially if you're using one that is gluten-free. Drain the pasta well and transfer to a large bowl.

Add the prepared sauce to the macaroni, mixing until the pasta is coated. Add salt and pepper to taste. Stir in ½ cup of the scallions. Scoop the macaroni into the prepared baking dish and sprinkle the top with a dusting of ground chipotle. Bake for 20 to 30 minutes, or until hot and starting to bubble around the edges. Remove from the oven. Top with the crushed chips, the remaining scallions, and cilantro. Serve the casserole right away.

Gluten-Free: Use a gluten-free macaroni. My favorite gluten-free pasta for this recipe is brown rice macaroni. It's also very good with quinoa macaroni.

Roasted Butternut Squash Casserole

Sometimes you just need a little roasted butternut squash in your mac and cheese, and that's when this recipe fits the bill. The roasted squash, onion, and garlic add a nice sweetness to this dish. Look for packages of peeled and cubed butternut squash in the grocery store, which makes the prep a lot easier.

Serves 4

12 ounces peeled and cubed butternut squash (2 cups)

1 medium sweet onion, thinly sliced

6 cloves garlic, sliced in half

1 to 2 tablespoons olive oil

Fine sea salt and freshly ground black pepper to taste

8 ounces dried macaroni

1 recipe Cheesy Sauce (page 178), using the white cheesy sauce variation

1 recipe Buttery Crumb Topping (page 162)

Paprika or cayenne pepper, for garnish

Preheat the oven to 425°F. Line a large baking sheet with parchment paper or foil. Grease a 13 x 9-inch glass or ceramic baking dish.

On the prepared baking sheet, combine the squash cubes, onion, and garlic. Drizzle with the oil and toss to coat. Add a pinch of salt and pepper and toss again. Roast for 25 to 30 minutes, or until the squash is tender and lightly browned.

Meanwhile, in a large pot of lightly salted boiling water, add the macaroni and cook according to package directions until al dente. Don't overcook the pasta, especially if you're using one that is gluten-free. Drain the pasta well and transfer to a large bowl. Reduce the oven temperature to 400°F once the squash is done.

Add the prepared sauce to the cooked macaroni, mixing until the pasta is coated. Add the roasted squash, onion, and garlic. Add salt and pepper to taste. Scoop the mixture into the prepared baking dish. Sprinkle the crumb topping over the top of the casserole, along with a dusting of paprika. Bake for 20 to 30 minutes, or until the

(recipe continues)

casserole is hot and the top is lightly browned. Remove from the oven and serve hot.

Tip: You can peel and cube a whole squash instead of buying it prepared. You can roast it all and then measure out 2 cups to use in the recipe. The extra roasted squash will keep well in the refrigerator for a couple of days.

Gluten-Free: Use a gluten-free macaroni, as well as gluten-free panko breadcrumbs in the topping. My favorite gluten-free pasta for this recipe is brown rice macaroni.

Baked Penne with Pumpkin Cream Sauce

Pumpkin is always a fall favorite, although you can enjoy this dish anytime of the year. The sauce has a hint of sweetness from the pumpkin but also a nice savory flavor from the sage and onions. I think this dish has become one of my daughter's favorites.

Serves 4 to 6

12 ounces dried penne

1 tablespoon olive oil

1 medium sweet onion, cut in half and thinly sliced

3 large cloves garlic, pressed or minced

1½ cups plain unsweetened soymilk or almond milk, plus more as needed

1 (15-ounce) can puréed pumpkin (not pumpkin pie mix)

5 tablespoons nutritional yeast flakes

¼ cup raw unsalted cashews, soaked for at least 2 hours and drained

1¼ teaspoons fine sea salt

1 teaspoon dried rubbed sage

¾ teaspoon freshly grated nutmeg

Salt and freshly ground black pepper to taste

1 recipe Buttery Crumb Topping (page 162), prepared without nutritional yeast flakes

Preheat the oven to 400°F. Grease an 8-inch square glass or ceramic baking dish.

In a large pot of lightly salted boiling water, add the penne and cook according to package directions until al dente. Don't overcook the pasta, especially if you're using one that is gluten-free. Drain the pasta well and transfer to a large bowl.

While the pasta is cooking, prepare the sauce. In a large cast-iron skillet, heat the oil over medium-high heat and sauté the onion until soft. Add the garlic and cook a few more minutes. Remove from the heat.

In a blender, purée the onion mixture, soymilk, pumpkin, nutritional yeast, cashews, salt, sage, and nutmeg. Blend until the mixture is super-smooth and velvety, and no traces of nuts remain. If the sauce is too thick to blend, you can add up to an additional ½ cup of nondairy milk.

Add the pumpkin sauce to the pasta, stirring until the pasta is well coated. Add salt and pepper to taste. Scoop the mixture into the prepared baking dish. Sprinkle the crumb topping over the

(recipe continues)

top of the casserole. Bake for 20 to 25 minutes, or until the casserole is hot and the top is lightly browned. Remove from the oven and serve hot.

Tip: If you're using a high-speed blender, you can skip the soaking step for the cashews and just use them dry. Add a little extra water to blend if needed.

Variation: Substitute fresh or dried rosemary for the sage.

Gluten-Free: Use a gluten-free pasta, such as brown rice, as well as gluten-free panko breadcrumbs in the topping. My favorite gluten-free pasta for this recipe is brown rice penne.

Creamy Spinach Florentine

Ever since I was a child, I have adored creamed spinach. This casserole totally reminds me of the stuffed spinach crêpes I would order as a teenager at this little crêpe restaurant near our house. I could never get enough of them. This casserole doesn't disappoint, with a luscious creamy sauce, spinach, and some dry sherry thrown in for good measure.

Serves 4

8 ounces dried shell pasta or macaroni

1 (10-ounce) bag frozen spinach, thawed

1 recipe Almost Alfredo Sauce (page 180)

3 to 4 tablespoons dry sherry, or to taste

1 tablespoon plus 2 teaspoons Dijon mustard

2 tablespoons nutritional yeast flakes

1 teaspoon granulated onion

¾ teaspoon freshly grated nutmeg

Fine sea salt and freshly ground black pepper to taste

Preheat the oven to 400°F. Grease an 8-inch square glass or ceramic baking dish.

In a large pot of lightly salted boiling water, add the pasta and cook according to package directions until al dente. Don't overcook the pasta, especially if you're using one that is gluten-free. Drain the pasta well and transfer to a large bowl.

Drain most of the liquid out of the spinach by gently squeezing it, but don't squeeze it completely dry. Add the spinach to the pasta, along with the sauce, mixing until the pasta is thickly coated. Add the sherry, Dijon mustard, nutritional yeast, granulated onion, and nutmeg, stirring well. Add salt and pepper, and adjust seasonings to taste. Scoop the pasta mixture into the prepared baking dish. Bake for 20 to 30 minutes, or until hot and slightly bubbly around the edges. Remove from the oven and serve.

Gluten-Free: Use a gluten-free oat flour in the sauce and gluten-free pasta (my favorite here is brown rice macaroni).

Truffled Cauliflower Mac

Sometimes you can never have enough truffle—or macaroni. This dish is for those times. It has a very rich flavor, with a creamy truffle sauce, steamed cauliflower, and a panko topping. If you happen to have a fresh truffle, you can go crazy and shave a few ultra-thin slices into the sauce before baking.

Serves 4

8 ounces dried macaroni

½ head cauliflower, cut into small florets

1 recipe Almost Alfredo Sauce (page 180), using the truffle variation

Truffle salt or fine sea salt and freshly ground black pepper to taste

2 recipes Buttery Crumb Topping (page 162)

Truffle oil, for garnish (optional)

Preheat the oven to 400°F. Grease a 13 x 9-inch glass or ceramic baking dish.

In a large pot of lightly salted boiling water, add the macaroni and cook according to package directions until tender. When the pasta is about 2 minutes away from being done, add the cauliflower to the boiling pasta water. You want the cauliflower to be just fork-tender and the noodles to be al dente. Drain the pasta and cauliflower well and transfer to a large bowl.

Add the prepared sauce to the cooked macaroni and cauliflower, mixing until the pasta is coated. Add salt and pepper to taste. Scoop the macaroni into the prepared baking dish. Sprinkle the crumb mixture over the top of the casserole. Bake for 20 to 30 minutes, or until the top is nicely browned and the casserole is heated through. Remove from the oven, drizzle the top of the casserole with a little truffle oil, if desired, and serve.

Variation: To make a straight truffle mac casserole, simply omit the cauliflower.

Gluten-Free: Use a gluten-free macaroni, such as brown rice macaroni, as well as gluten-free panko breadcrumbs in the topping.

Baked Penne and Wild Mushrooms

This mushroom casserole is a new family favorite, which isn't too surprising, as we tend to love any dish that's full of wild mushrooms and a creamy, silky sauce. Although I use chanterelles in the recipe, you can also use oyster, shiitake, or even cremini mushrooms.

Serves 4

1 tablespoon nonhydrogenated vegan margarine
    or olive oil
1 pound chanterelle or other wild mushrooms,
    cleaned and sliced
6 cloves garlic, minced or pressed, divided
6 ounces dried penne
2 cups plain unsweetened soymilk
½ cup raw unsalted cashews, soaked for at least
    2 hours and drained
¼ cup nutritional yeast flakes
¼ cup cornstarch
3 tablespoons Marsala
1 teaspoon fine sea salt, or more to taste
1 teaspoon truffle oil (optional)
1 cup water
½ teaspoon freshly grated nutmeg, or more to taste
Freshly ground black pepper to taste
1 recipe Buttery Crumb Topping (page 162)
¼ cup minced fresh parsley

Preheat the oven to 400°F. Grease an 8-inch square glass or ceramic baking dish.

In a large skillet over medium-high heat, place the margarine. Once it's melted and hot, add the mushrooms and cook, stirring as needed, until the mushrooms have released all of their liquid and the liquid has cooked off, for about 5 minutes. Add 4 of the cloves of garlic to the skillet and cook until the mushrooms are tender, for another 5 minutes. Remove from the heat, but keep the mushrooms in the pan.

While the mushrooms are cooking, cook the pasta in a large pot of lightly salted boiling water according to package directions until tender. Don't overcook the pasta, especially if you're using one that is gluten-free. Drain the pasta well and transfer to a large bowl.

In the jar of a blender, combine the soymilk, cashews, nutritional yeast, cornstarch, Marsala, remaining 2 cloves of garlic, salt, and truffle oil, if using. Blend for several minutes or until the sauce is completely smooth and there are no remaining little bits of nuts. If there's room in your blender, add the cup of water and blend again until smooth. Otherwise, you can whisk the water into the pan when you add the sauce.

Add the cashew sauce to the mushrooms in the skillet and whisk in the water if you haven't already added it. Cook over medium-high heat, stirring constantly, until the sauce gets very thick, for about 5 minutes. Sprinkle in the nutmeg and add the pepper to taste, mixing well. Add the reserved pasta and mix well. Adjust seasonings to taste.

Place the pasta mixture into the prepared baking dish. Sprinkle the top with the prepared crumb topping and sprinkle the minced parsley over the crumbs. Bake for 20 to 25 minutes, or until the casserole is hot and the crumb topping is lightly golden.

Tip: If you're using a high-speed blender, you can skip the soaking step for the cashews and just use them dry. Add a little extra water to blend if needed.

Gluten-Free: Use a gluten-free macaroni, such as brown rice macaroni, as well as gluten-free panko bread-crumbs in the topping.

Apple Cinnamon Kugel

I grew up on kugel at holidays and family gatherings. It's a sweet Jewish casserole with noodles, held together with a creamy filling. I absolutely adored it. It's traditionally made with a lot of butter, and even more eggs and dairy, so it took me a long time to veganize the recipe and get it just right, but I did it! And the best part of all is that it is even better than the original.

Serves 4 as a side dish

8 ounces dried rotelle pasta, bow-tie pasta, or any type of noodle that resembles wide, flat egg noodles

1½ (12.3-ounce) boxes firm or extra-firm silken tofu (such as Mori-Nu)

½ cup vegan sour cream

¼ cup unsweetened applesauce

¾ cup plus 1½ tablespoons granulated sugar, divided

3 tablespoons cornstarch

¾ teaspoon ground cinnamon, plus more for sprinkling

2 teaspoons pure vanilla extract

1 crisp apple, peeled, cored, and thinly sliced (such as Granny Smith)

⅓ cup raisins, or more to taste

Preheat the oven to 350°F. Grease an 8-inch square glass or ceramic baking dish with shortening.

In a large pot of lightly salted boiling water, add the pasta and cook according to package directions until al dente. Don't overcook the pasta, especially if you're using one that is gluten-free. Drain the pasta well and transfer to a large bowl.

In the bowl of a food processor or a blender jar, combine the tofu, sour cream, applesauce, ¾ cup sugar, cornstarch, cinnamon, and vanilla and blend until it's completely smooth. This might take a minute or two. Stop the machine and scrape down the sides as necessary.

Transfer the sour cream mixture to the bowl with the pasta. Add the apples and raisins, mixing well. Scoop the mixture into the prepared baking dish, smoothing the top as best as you can. Sprinkle the top with the remaining 1½ tablespoons granulated sugar and some ground cinnamon to taste. Bake for 60 minutes, or until the top is golden brown and slightly firm to the touch and the kugel has puffed up a little.

(recipe continues)

Let the pan cool on a wire rack before slicing into squares and serving. The kugel can be served warm or cold.

Tip: The kugel is wonderful refrigerated overnight before serving, as it has the chance to firm up, making it much easier to slice. It will keep refrigerated for several days—if it doesn't get eaten sooner.

Variation: If you prefer your kugel sweeter, you can increase the sugar to taste.

Gluten-Free: Use gluten-free noodles in this recipe. My personal favorite here is quinoa rotelle. If using gluten-free noodles, make sure to reheat leftovers in the microwave to soften the noodles.

Sweet Potato Pie Kugel

Although this might sound like one wacky casserole, this kugel is super-delicious, with all of the nice warm flavors of a sweet potato pie. Cinnamon, ginger, and allspice add a spicy note to the filling, and brown sugar lends a sweet caramel flavor. One bite and you may find yourself asking, "Why didn't my bubbe make this kugel?"

Serves 4 as a side dish

8 ounces dried rotelle pasta, bow-tie pasta, or any type of noodle that resembles wide, flat egg noodles

1 (12.3-ounce) box firm or extra-firm silken tofu (such as Mori-Nu)

1 cup cooked and mashed sweet potato

½ cup vegan sour cream

1¼ cups firmly packed light brown sugar

3 tablespoons cornstarch

1½ teaspoons ground cinnamon, plus more for sprinkling

1 teaspoon ground allspice

1 teaspoon ground ginger

⅓ cup raisins, or more to taste

1½ tablespoons granulated sugar

Preheat the oven to 350°F. Grease an 8-inch square glass or ceramic baking dish with shortening.

In a large pot of lightly salted boiling water, add the pasta and cook according to package directions until al dente. Don't overcook the pasta, especially if you're using one that is gluten-free. Drain the pasta well and transfer to a large bowl.

In the bowl of a food processor or a blender jar, combine the tofu, mashed sweet potato, sour cream, brown sugar, cornstarch, cinnamon, allspice, and ginger and blend until it's completely smooth. This might take a minute or two. Stop the machine and scrape down the sides as necessary.

Transfer the sweet potato mixture to the bowl with the pasta. Add the raisins, mixing well. Scoop the mixture into the prepared baking dish, smoothing the top as best as you can. Sprinkle the top with the granulated sugar and some cinnamon. Bake for 60 to 75 minutes, or until the top is nicely browned and slightly firm to the touch and the kugel has puffed up a little.

(recipe continues)

Let the pan cool on a wire rack before slicing into squares and serving. The kugel can be served warm or cold.

Tip: The kugel is wonderful refrigerated overnight before serving. If serving warm the next day, reheat it in the microwave. The regular oven tends to dry it out. The casserole will keep refrigerated for several days—if it doesn't get eaten sooner.

Gluten-Free: Use gluten-free noodles in this recipe. My personal favorite here is quinoa rotelle.

Chapter Five

• • •

Vegetable Casseroles

Italian-Style Stuffed Swiss Chard

This stuffed Swiss chard casserole offers a nice meaty texture thanks to the bulked-up rice filling, almost like an Italian twist on stuffed grape leaves. If you can't find large chard leaves, you can use smaller leaves and overlap them slightly. Also, make sure to use sweet white rice flour here, as regular rice flour won't work.

Serves 4

2 cups TSP or TVP granules, preferably organic

1½ cups boiling water

1 to 2 bunches chard (try to find nice big leaves in a big bunch), any variety

1 tablespoon granulated onion

3 tablespoons nutritional yeast flakes

2 teaspoons sweet paprika

2 teaspoons granulated garlic

1 teaspoon red pepper flakes

2 teaspoons fennel seeds, crushed with a mortar and pestle

¼ cup low-sodium tamari or soy sauce

2 cloves garlic, finely minced or pressed

2 cups cooked long-grain white rice

3 tablespoons tomato paste

3½ cups Quick Tomato Basil Sauce (page 185) or store-bought sauce, divided

2 tablespoons sweet white rice flour

Preheat the oven to 400°F. Grease an 8-inch square glass or ceramic baking dish.

In a large bowl, combine the TSP and boiling water. Cover tightly with plastic wrap or foil and let sit for 10 minutes to reconstitute.

While the TSP is reconstituting, fold the chard leaves in half and carefully cut out the thick stem from the center of each leaf. You may need to trim the ends from the leaves so that each piece is about 7 inches long and 5 inches wide. If you can't find large leaves, use whatever size you can find and remove the center stems of the leaves.

Bring a large pot of water to a boil over high heat. Add the chard leaves and cook for 10 to 15 seconds. Carefully remove the leaves and rinse with cold water. Spread the leaves out on a clean kitchen towel and blot to remove excess moisture.

Add the granulated onion, nutritional yeast, paprika, granulated garlic, red pepper flakes, crushed fennel seed, tamari, garlic, cooked rice, and tomato paste to the reconstituted TSP, mixing well. Stir in 2 tablespoons of tomato basil sauce and mix well. Sprinkle the sweet white rice flour over the mixture and mix well. Using your hands, gently squeeze (but do not mash) the mixture together, which will activate the sweet white rice flour to make the mixture stick together.

Take a small handful of filling, gently squeeze it into a small log or oval, and place it onto the bottom of a chard leaf and roll up like a jellyroll, carefully tucking in the sides if you can. Repeat with the remaining leaves. If your leaves are very small, simply overlap two leaves at a time, fill, and roll.

Spoon 1 cup of the tomato basil sauce on the bottom of the prepared pan. Arrange the rolls, seam-side down, in a single layer over the tomato sauce. Pour the rest of the sauce evenly over the top of the casserole. Bake for 30 minutes, or until the rolls and sauce are hot. Cool for 5 to 10 minutes and serve.

Baked Sweet Potato and Apple Casserole

Have you ever had one of those Thanksgiving dishes that you dream about all year? I have been making this casserole for Thanksgiving for the past twenty-three years. It has become a true family favorite, with the perfect balance of apples, sweet potatoes, and spices. It's also extra delicious and easy if you bake the casserole the day before and then reheat, covered with foil, until warmed through. I suggest making this casserole more often than once a year. If you want to make it extra special, you can melt some vegan marshmallows on the top right before serving.

Serves 6 to 8

4 to 5 large sweet potatoes (about 4½ pounds)

6 medium green apples (about 2½ to 3 pounds), peeled, cored, and thinly sliced

1¾ cups apple cider or juice (spiced or plain)

1¼ cups firmly packed light brown sugar, plus more as needed

½ teaspoon ground cinnamon, plus more as needed

¼ teaspoon ground allspice

2 tablespoons cornstarch

2 tablespoons cool water

Freshly grated nutmeg

Preheat the oven to 400°F. Grease a 13 x 9-inch glass or ceramic baking dish.

Bake or microwave the sweet potatoes until tender. Set aside to cool, then peel and cut into ½-inch slices.

In a large, deep skillet, combine the apple slices, apple cider, brown sugar, cinnamon, and allspice. Cook over medium heat until the mixture comes to a simmer. Reduce the heat slightly and simmer for 10 minutes, or until the apples are soft and tender.

In a small bowl, whisk together the cornstarch and water until smooth. Whisking continuously, stir it into the apple mixture. Continue cooking and stirring for a couple of minutes, until the liquid has thickened. Remove from the heat.

In the prepared baking dish, layer the sweet potato slices and the cooked apple mixture (including the liquid), starting with the sweet potatoes and ending with the apples. Lightly sprinkle the top of the casserole with a little more brown sugar and a dusting of cinnamon and nutmeg.

Bake for 35 to 40 minutes, or until the juices are thick and bubbling and the top is lightly browned.

Tip: This casserole is also really good with crumbled gingersnaps on top, or make it even jazzier with some vegan marshmallows.

Truffled Potato Gratin

If you are a truffle fan, then this might just be the ultimate comfort food dish: creamy, melt-in-your-mouth potatoes with a silky cashew-based truffle cream sauce. Decadence and deliciousness all wrapped up in the same package.

Serves 6 to 9 as a side dish

2 cups cool water

1 cup raw unsalted cashews, soaked
    for at least 2 hours and drained

2 cloves garlic

1 tablespoon truffle oil, plus more for drizzling

1 teaspoon fine sea salt

3 extra-large russet potatoes (about 2½ pounds),
    peeled, rinsed, and sliced ultra-thin,
    preferably with a mandoline

Sprig fresh rosemary

Preheat the oven to 400°F. Grease an 8-inch square glass or ceramic baking dish with shortening.

In the jar of a blender, combine the water, cashews, garlic, truffle oil, and salt. Blend until the mixture is completely smooth and there are no traces of nuts.

Evenly layer the potatoes in the prepared baking dish. Pour the blended sauce over the top, making sure to submerge the potatoes in the sauce. Place the sprig of rosemary decoratively in the center of the potatoes.

Cover the casserole with aluminum foil and bake for 75 to 90 minutes, or until the potatoes are soft and tender when a knife is inserted into the center and the top is puffed up.

Let the potatoes cool for 15 minutes before serving. Just before serving, very lightly drizzle the top with additional truffle oil for an extra kick.

Tip: If you're using a high-speed blender, you can skip the soaking step for the cashews and just use them dry. Add a little extra water to blend if needed.

Variation: If you can't find truffle oil, you can omit it from the recipe and make a plain potato gratin. Just add 2 tablespoons nutritional yeast flakes to the sauce.

Summer Corn Custard

I asked my good friend Bryanna Clark Grogan, who is a fabulous vegan chef and cookbook author, if she had a special casserole recipe that she loved and wanted to share. She did, and she couldn't have picked a better summer recipe.

Serves 4

12 ounces firm or extra-firm silken tofu
    (such as Mori-Nu)
2 tablespoons plus 1 teaspoon finely ground
    yellow cornmeal
1 tablespoon nutritional yeast flakes
¾ teaspoon salt
¼ teaspoon ground turmeric
¼ teaspoon baking powder
1 tablespoon olive oil or nonhydrogenated
    vegan margarine
1 small yellow onion, minced
1 clove garlic, minced or pressed
½ red or green bell pepper, chopped
2 cups fresh or frozen corn kernels, thawed if
    frozen, coarsely chopped in a food processor
1 to 2 tablespoons chopped fresh herbs,
    such as tarragon, basil, parsley, cilantro,
    or oregano

Preheat the oven to 350°F. Grease a 9-inch glass or ceramic pie dish.

In a food processor, blend together the tofu, cornmeal, nutritional yeast, salt, turmeric, and baking powder. Blend until very smooth.

In a large skillet, heat the oil over medium-high heat. Add the onion and cook until it's beginning to soften. Add the garlic, bell pepper, and corn. Sauté the mixture until the pepper is softened. Remove from the heat.

Fold the cooked veggies and fresh herbs into the tofu batter in a medium bowl. Transfer the mixture into the prepared baking dish.

Bake for 35 minutes, or until the custard is set. Serve warm.

Tip: If you don't have finely ground cornmeal (also called corn flour), you can use 4½ teaspoons cornstarch instead, but the cornmeal does add extra corn flavor.

This is best made with fresh seasonal corn, but it is still delicious using frozen corn.

Gluten-Free: Use gluten-free cornmeal in the recipe.

Eggplant Parm

Eggplant Parm is one of those classic Italian dishes, the kind that evokes memories of naugahyde booths and dimly lit restaurants. For me though, it's more than just the memories. It's the creamy, melt-in-your-mouth flavors of tomato, roasted eggplant, and cheese. You'd never guess that this version is both gluten-free and vegan.

Serves 4

Salt, for sprinkling

About 4 very small eggplants, or 1 large
   eggplant (between 1 and 1¼ pounds),
   cut into ¼- to ½-inch slices

½ cup plain unsweetened soymilk or
   other nondairy milk

¼ cup cornstarch

1½ cups panko breadcrumbs

3 tablespoons nutritional yeast flakes

Freshly ground black pepper to taste

2 tablespoons olive oil, plus more as needed

1 recipe Quick Tomato Basil Sauce (page 185),
   or 4 cups store-bought tomato sauce

1 cup shredded vegan mozzarella

Sprinkle salt on both sides of each slice of eggplant and set aside on a plate for 15 to 20 minutes. This will help remove any bitterness from the eggplant. You will notice that the eggplant is expelling little beads of water. That's what you want. Rinse the salt off the eggplant and pat dry with a towel.

Preheat the oven to 400°F. Grease an 8-inch square glass or ceramic baking dish.

In a shallow bowl, whisk together the soymilk and cornstarch. In a separate shallow bowl or on a plate, combine the panko, nutritional yeast, and a pinch of salt and a few grinds of black pepper.

Set a large cast-iron or nonstick skillet over medium-high heat. Swirl it around the pan. Coat the eggplant slices with the soymilk mixture, then thoroughly coat with the panko, making sure to evenly coat both sides. Place the eggplant slices in the skillet and cook without disturbing. Once the eggplant is nicely browned on one side, about 5 minutes, carefully flip the slices over and continue cooking until the second side is nicely browned. Remove the cooked eggplant slices to a clean plate or cutting board and set aside.

(recipe continues)

Repeat with the remaining eggplant, adding additional olive oil as needed.

In the prepared baking dish, cover the bottom with about one-third of the sauce. Top with a layer of half the eggplant slices and sprinkle with ⅓ cup cheese. Top with half the remaining sauce, the remaining eggplant slices, ⅓ cup cheese, and then the last of the sauce. Sprinkle the remaining ⅓ cup cheese on top of the casserole. Cover the baking dish with aluminum foil and bake for 30 minutes, or until the casserole is hot and the cheese has melted. Serve hot.

Variation: You can easily omit the cheese for a cheese-less version.

Gluten-Free: Use gluten-free panko breadcrumbs.

Green Bean Casserole

Many people cannot imagine a Thanksgiving dinner without their much-beloved green bean casserole, and for good reason. There's just something about the creamy sauce, the tender green beans, and that crispy onion topping. This is my vegan version of the classic casserole. It still has all of the creamy goodness that everyone expects, but everything is made from scratch, including the crispy onion topping.

Serves 4

Salt

1½ pounds fresh green beans, trimmed and cut into 2-inch pieces

1 recipe Cream of Mushroom Soup (page 168), prepared with an additional 2 teaspoons cornstarch

½ cup plain unsweetened soymilk or almond milk

2 cloves garlic, pressed or minced

1 tablespoon Marsala or sherry

½ teaspoon truffle oil

Freshly ground black pepper to taste

1 recipe Crispy Fried Onions (page 160)

Preheat the oven to 400°F. Grease an 9-inch glass or ceramic baking dish or deep 2 quart casserole dish.

Fill a large pot with hot water and bring to a rolling boil over high heat. Add a big pinch of salt and the beans to the water. Cover and cook for about 7 minutes. The beans should be bright green and just tender to the bite.

Drain the beans in a colander and rinse with cold water for several minutes to stop the cooking. Drain them well, shaking the colander to get off all the water.

Transfer the cooked green beans to a bowl. Stir in the prepared mushroom soup, soymilk, garlic, Marsala, and truffle oil. Add salt and pepper, and adjust seasonings to taste.

Scoop the green bean mixture into the prepared baking dish and top with the crispy onions. Bake for 15 to 20 minutes, or until the casserole is hot.

Mushroom-Spinach Quinoa Casserole

This is probably one of my favorite recipes. It's full of flavor and packs hearty protein from the quinoa. It makes a perfect dinner alongside a green salad.

Serves 4

1 tablespoon olive oil, plus more as needed

1 small yellow onion, diced

1 cup sliced cremini or shiitake mushrooms

2 cloves garlic, pressed or finely minced

5 ounces baby spinach

2 recipes Cream of Mushroom Soup (page 168)

3 cups cooked quinoa (see sidebar)

¼ teaspoon dried rubbed sage

Salt and freshly ground black pepper to taste

Preheat the oven to 400°F. Grease an 8-inch square glass or ceramic baking dish.

Heat the oil in a large skillet over medium heat. Add the onion, mushrooms, and garlic and cook, stirring, for about 10 minutes, or until the onions and mushrooms are softened and golden in color. Add the spinach and cook until just wilted.

In a large bowl, stir together the soup, cooked onion mixture, quinoa, and sage, mixing until everything is well combined. Add salt and pepper to taste. Transfer the mixture into the prepared baking dish. Bake for 20 to 30 minutes, or until hot and puffed, with a nice crust on top. Remove from the oven and serve hot.

Tip: If you like a lot of spinach, you can double the amount of spinach in the recipe.

Variation: One of my recipe testers likes to add sliced vegan sausages to this casserole. Thanks, Craig, for the great suggestion!

To cook quinoa, combine 1½ cups water with 1 cup well-rinsed quinoa in a medium saucepan. Give it a stir, bring it to a simmer, reduce the heat to low, cover, and let cook for 15 minutes. Turn off the heat and let it sit, covered, for another 5 minutes. This will yield about 3 cups cooked quinoa.

Roasted Tomatoes with Garlic and Breadcrumbs

Roasted tomatoes make an absolutely delicious side dish. You can double the recipe to serve more people, serve with pasta, or serve as a side dish to one of the pasta casseroles in this book. The dish is especially wonderful during the summer, when tomatoes are at their best. I like to serve bread alongside and dip it into the garlicky tomato juices.

Serves 4 as a side dish

2 to 3 tablespoons olive oil

4 cloves garlic, pressed or minced

4 large beefsteak tomatoes, sliced into
¼- to ⅓-inch slices

Salt and freshly ground black pepper to taste

1 recipe Buttery Crumb Topping (page 162),
prepared without garlic

Minced fresh basil or parsley, for garnish

Preheat the oven to 400°F. Grease an 8-inch square glass or ceramic baking dish.

In a small dish, mix together 2 to 3 tablespoons of olive oil and the minced garlic. Place a layer of tomatoes in the prepared baking dish and sprinkle with salt and pepper. Using a small spoon, drizzle a little bit of the garlic oil over each tomato, spreading it lightly over the tomato with the back of the spoon. Repeat with the remaining tomatoes, making another layer or two, as needed, drizzling each with garlic oil and sprinkling with salt and pepper. Bake for about 30 minutes, or until they are softened.

Carefully remove the baking dish from the oven and sprinkle the crumb topping evenly over the tomatoes, avoiding the juices in the corners. Return the tomatoes to the oven and bake for 15 more minutes, or until the crumbs are lightly browned. Sprinkle the tomatoes with the minced basil and serve.

Gluten-Free: Use gluten-free panko breadcrumbs in the topping.

Shiitake, Rice, and Green Bean Casserole

I love this casserole so much! It takes a few minutes longer to make than some of the other casseroles in this book, but it's so worth it. It reminds me a little bit of a Thanksgiving dish, held together with a creamy sauce. Leftovers are delicious too, and even more delectable when topped with freshly ground pepper and a little drizzle of truffle oil.

Serves 4 as a side dish

10 ounces fresh green beans, trimmed and cut into 1-inch pieces

2 recipes Cream of Mushroom Soup (page 168), made with the shiitake mushroom variation

2 cups cooked long-grain white or brown rice

1 cup diced Chicken-Style Soy Curls (page 166) or other store-bought vegan chicken

½ teaspoon dried rubbed sage

2 tablespoons dried chopped onion

1½ tablespoons tamari or soy sauce

2 tablespoons nutritional yeast flakes

Salt and freshly ground black pepper to taste

Preheat the oven to 400°F. Grease an 8-inch square glass or ceramic baking dish.

In a medium pot with a steamer insert, add water just to the level of the bottom of the steamer. Bring the water to a boil. Add the green beans to the steamer, cover, reduce the heat, and steam for 5 minutes, or just until tender. Transfer the green beans to a cutting board to cool slightly.

In a large bowl, combine the green beans, mushroom soup, rice, Soy Curls, sage, onion, tamari, and nutritional yeast, mixing until everything is well coated. Add salt and pepper to taste. Scoop the mixture into the prepared baking dish. Bake for 20 to 30 minutes, or until hot, with a nice crust on top. Remove from the oven and serve hot.

Variation: For an all-vegetable version, you can omit the Soy Curls. If you want to jazz things up a little further, lightly drizzle the top of the baked casserole with truffle oil.

Gluten-Free: Use a gluten-free vegan chicken substitute (such as Beyond Meat or Soy Curls) and gluten-free tamari.

Spinach Artichoke Casserole

I love artichoke dip and had been dreaming about a casserole version for quite a while. This casserole is quick to make and is certainly much healthier than a big dish of artichoke dip.

Serves 4

8 ounces dried penne, macaroni, or rotelle

1 (12-ounce) box firm or extra-firm silken tofu (such as Mori-Nu)

½ cup plus 2 tablespoons nutritional yeast flakes

¼ cup plus 2 tablespoons plain unsweetened soymilk or other nondairy milk, plus more as needed

4 cloves garlic, minced or pressed

1 tablespoon Dijon mustard

1½ teaspoons fine sea salt, or more to taste

1 teaspoon granulated onion

1 teaspoon granulated garlic

Freshly ground black pepper to taste

1 (16-ounce) bag frozen spinach, thawed and squeezed dry

1 (13.75-ounce) can artichoke hearts, drained and sliced in half

Preheat the oven to 400°F. Grease an 8-inch square glass or ceramic baking dish.

In a large pot of lightly salted boiling water, add the pasta and cook according to package directions until tender. Don't overcook the pasta, especially if you're using one that is gluten-free. Drain the pasta well and transfer to a large bowl.

In the bowl of a food processor, combine the tofu, nutritional yeast, soymilk, fresh garlic, mustard, salt, granulated onion, granulated garlic, and a few grinds of freshly ground pepper. Blend the mixture until completely smooth. If the mixture is hard to blend, you can add another tablespoon or two of soymilk. Add the spinach and pulse a few times until mixed in and chopped. Add the artichokes and pulse a couple of times until chunky.

Pour the spinach and artichoke sauce over the cooked pasta, mixing until the pasta is coated. Adjust seasonings to taste. Scoop into the prepared baking dish and bake for 30 minutes, or until the top is puffed and the casserole is bubbly around the edges. Remove from the oven and serve.

Tip: I really like this casserole with a sprinkle of cayenne pepper on top.

Gluten-Free: Use a gluten-free pasta.

Chickpeas with Rice, Dill, and Tomatoes

I first made a version of this casserole to bring to a potluck at a friend's house. It got high marks, especially since it was different from the usual suspects of potluck casseroles. Plus, it has deliciously fresh flavors of the Mediterranean: dill, tahini, garlic, tomatoes, and chickpeas.

Serves 4 to 6

1 tablespoon olive oil

1 medium sweet or yellow onion, diced

3 cloves garlic, pressed or finely minced

2½ cups cooked short- or long-grain brown rice (see sidebar)

2 (15-ounce) cans chickpeas, drained and rinsed (3 cups)

¼ cup minced fresh dill, plus more for garnish

¼ cup minced fresh parsley

2 Roma tomatoes, diced

1 recipe Creamy Tahini Sauce (page 181), divided

Salt and freshly ground black pepper to taste

½ lemon

Preheat the oven to 400°F. Grease an 8-inch square or 11 x 7-inch glass or ceramic baking dish.

Heat the oil in a large skillet over medium-high heat. Add the onion and garlic and cook, stirring, for about 5 minutes, or until the onions just start to get some color.

In a large bowl, combine the cooked onion mixture, rice, chickpeas, dill, parsley, tomatoes, and half of the tahini sauce. Mix well. If the mixture seems too dry, add a touch more sauce as needed. Add salt and pepper to taste. Spread the mixture into the prepared baking dish and cover the top with foil. Bake for 10 minutes. Carefully remove the foil and continue baking for 20 more minutes, or until hot.

Squeeze half of a lemon over the top of the casserole, catching any seeds, and then sprinkle with a little minced dill before serving. Serve the remaining tahini sauce on the side.

To make 2½ cups brown rice, cook 1 cup short- or long-grain brown rice with 1½ cups water. My favorite way to make it is in a rice cooker. If making the rice on the stove top, combine 1 cup rinsed rice and 1½ cups water in a medium saucepan. Bring to a simmer, cover tightly, reduce heat to low, and cook for 35 to 40 minutes, or until the rice is tender and the water is absorbed. Let the cooked rice sit, covered, for 5 minutes before using.

Zucchini Basil Casserole with Buttery Crumb Topping

When I was a child, I would spend summers at my best friend's grandparents' farm. They were magical summers, and one of my favorite dishes was a squash casserole that her grandma Edna would make. This is my modern spin on that buttery casserole with the crispy topping.

Serves 2 to 4

1½ pounds zucchini

⅓ cup thinly sliced fresh basil

2 tablespoons nonhydrogenated vegan margarine, melted

¾ teaspoon fine sea salt

Freshly ground black pepper to taste

1 recipe Buttery Crumb Topping (page 162)

Preheat the oven to 400°F. Grease an 8-inch square glass or ceramic baking dish.

Trim off the ends of the zucchini and shred the zucchini on the large holes of a box grater into a medium bowl. Add the basil, melted margarine, and salt, tossing until everything is coated. Add a few grinds of fresh black pepper.

Spread the zucchini mixture evenly into the prepared baking dish. Cover with foil and bake for 20 minutes. Carefully remove the foil and evenly sprinkle the crumb topping over the zucchini. Return to the oven uncovered and bake for another 10 to 15 minutes, or until the top is browned and crispy.

Gluten-Free: Use gluten-free panko breadcrumbs in the topping.

Mediterranean Stuffed Cabbage Rolls

This recipe was loosely adapted from one of my favorite vegan chefs, Tanya Petrovna from Native Foods. She had the fantastic idea of adding sauerkraut to the filling, which makes these delicious rolls completely irresistible! They are super-healthy too, and full of the fresh flavors of the Mediterranean. The flavor gets even better after a day or two in the fridge.

Serves about 6

1 very large head or 2 small heads green cabbage, core removed

1 tablespoon olive oil

1 large yellow onion, diced

4 cloves garlic, minced or pressed

3 cups cooked quinoa (see sidebar on page 124)

1 (15-ounce) can chickpeas, drained and rinsed (1½ cups)

1 cup drained sauerkraut

¾ cup minced fresh parsley, divided

¼ cup drained capers

¼ cup minced fresh dill, plus more for garnish

2 teaspoons granulated onion

2 teaspoons granulated garlic

Salt and freshly ground black pepper to taste

1 (28-ounce) can diced tomatoes, preferably organic, undrained and puréed

1 large lemon, cut in half

Lemon slices, for serving (optional)

Fit a large pot with a steamer insert and add water just to the bottom of the steamer. Bring the water to a simmer. Place the cabbage in the steamer, cover, and steam the whole head(s) of cabbage for 40 to 45 minutes, or until the cabbage is tender and cooked all the way through when pierced with a sharp knife. Turn off the heat, remove the lid, and let the cabbage cool down. Once the cabbage is somewhat cool, carefully slice the very bottom off the cabbage, which will help release the leaves.

Preheat the oven to 400°F. Grease a deep 13 x 9-inch glass or ceramic baking dish.

While the cabbage is steaming, in a large skillet or deep pot over medium-high heat, warm the oil. Stir in the onion and garlic and sauté until the onion is softened and golden in color. Add the quinoa, chickpeas, sauerkraut, ½ cup parsley, capers, dill, granulated onion, and granulated garlic and stir to combine. Turn off the heat. Add salt and pepper to taste.

(recipe continues)

On a cutting board, place a steamed cabbage leaf rib-side down. Place a large spoonful of the filling in the center, fold in the sides, and roll up. Repeat with the remaining leaves and filling. Place the rolled cabbage leaves in the prepared baking dish, packing them in as tightly as you need to. If you have small leftover cabbage leaves, you can tuck them down in between the rolls. Once the baking dish is full, pour the puréed tomatoes evenly over the top of the rolls. Cover with foil and bake for 20 minutes. Carefully remove the foil and bake for another 25 minutes, or until the rolls are hot and tender. Let sit for 10 minutes. When ready to serve, squeeze some fresh lemon juice on top, catching any seeds, and sprinkle with the remaining fresh parsley or some dill and serve. If desired, serve the cabbage rolls with lemon slices on the side.

Tip: The cabbage rolls are excellent as leftovers, reheated in the microwave. My friend Kittee shared her grandmother's secret for freezing the cabbage whole to tenderize it, instead of steaming it. Simply remove the bottom core from the cabbage and freeze overnight until solid. Defrost in a bowl or under warm water. Use as directed in the recipe.

Mushroom and Quinoa Enchiladas

My husband fell in love with these enchiladas and their deliciously smoky flavor. The texture is great too, thanks to the hearty mushrooms and quinoa.

Serves 4

2 tablespoons olive oil, divided

18 ounces cremini or button mushrooms, sliced

2 cups cooked quinoa (see sidebar on page 124)

1 cup thinly sliced scallions, divided

½ teaspoon smoked paprika

½ teaspoon dried oregano

1 medium yellow onion, finely diced

3 cloves garlic, minced or pressed

10 corn tortillas

1 recipe Everyday Enchilada Sauce (page 183), or 4 cups store-bought enchilada sauce

Preheat the oven to 400°F. Grease a 13 x 9-inch glass or ceramic baking dish.

In a large skillet, place 1 tablespoon oil and heat over medium-high heat. Add the mushrooms and sauté for 15 to 20 minutes, or until the mushrooms are soft. Remove them to a large bowl and stir in the quinoa, half of the scallions, and the smoked paprika and oregano.

Place the remaining tablespoon of oil in the skillet and heat over medium-high heat. Add the onion and garlic and sauté for 10 to 15 minutes, or until softened and lightly browned. Add the cooked onion to the mushroom mixture.

Microwave the tortillas on high for 30 seconds. This softens them and makes them more pliable. Coat the bottom of the prepared baking dish with a ladleful of enchilada sauce. Pour the remaining enchilada sauce into a large shallow bowl and dip the tortillas into the enchilada sauce to lightly coat. Working with one tortilla at a time, place the tortilla down on a cutting board and spoon ¼ to ⅓ cup of filling on top. Roll the tortilla over the filling and place the enchiladas in the pan, seam-side down. Repeat with the remaining tortillas and filling. If you have leftover
(recipe continues)

filling, simply scatter it over the enchiladas. Pour the remaining enchilada sauce evenly over the top, covering the tortillas as best as you can.

Cover the baking dish with foil and bake for 40 minutes. Remove the foil and continue baking for another 10 to 15 minutes, or until the tortillas are tender when pierced with a knife and the sauce is bubbly around the edges. Garnish with the remaining scallions and serve.

Variation: Add ½ cup shredded vegan cheese to the top of the casserole before baking, if desired.

Zucchini, Corn, and Black Bean Enchiladas

Nothing screams "casserole" like a bubbly pan of enchiladas! These enchiladas are a hearty and healthy version, stuffed with fresh zucchini, corn, and black beans, with lots of zesty sauce.

Serves 4

1 tablespoon olive oil

1 small yellow onion, diced

2 small to medium zucchini, shredded on the large holes of a box grater

3 to 4 cloves garlic, minced or pressed

1 cup fresh or frozen corn kernels, thawed and drained if frozen

1 (15-ounce) can black beans, drained and rinsed

1 cup cooked quinoa or brown rice

8 to 10 corn tortillas, as needed

1 recipe Everyday Enchilada Sauce (page 183), or 4 cups store-bought enchilada sauce

⅓ to ½ cup thinly sliced scallions, for garnish

Minced fresh cilantro, for garnish

Preheat the oven to 400°F. Grease a 13 x 9-inch glass or ceramic baking dish.

In a large skillet, place the oil and heat over medium-high heat. Add the onion and zucchini and cook, stirring as needed, until the onion and zucchini soften and the onion begins to color, for about 10 minutes. Add the garlic and cook for another 2 minutes. Add the corn, black beans, and quinoa, stirring well, and cook until the filling is warm.

Microwave the tortillas on high for 30 seconds. This softens them and makes them more pliable. Coat the bottom of the prepared baking dish with a ladleful of enchilada sauce. Pour the remaining enchilada sauce into a large shallow bowl and dip the tortillas into the enchilada sauce to lightly coat. Working with one tortilla at a time, place the tortilla down on a cutting board and spoon ¼ to ⅓ cup of filling on top. Roll the tortilla over the filling and place the enchiladas in the pan, seam-side down. Repeat with the remaining tortillas and filling. If you have leftover filling, simply scatter it over the enchiladas. Pour the remaining enchilada sauce evenly over the top, covering the tortillas as best as you can.

(recipe continues)

Cover the baking dish with foil and bake for 40 minutes. Remove the foil and continue baking for another 10 to 15 minutes, or until the tortillas are tender when pierced with a knife and the sauce is bubbly around the edges. Garnish with scallions and cilantro and serve.

Tip: If you want to keep the foil from sticking to the top of your enchiladas, spray it with a little oil or lightly grease it before covering the casserole.

Variation: For a cheesy casserole, sprinkle the top of the casserole with shredded vegan cheese before covering and baking.

Italian Stuffed Peppers with Fennel and Garlic

One bite of these stuffed peppers and I'm reminded of the ones that my husband used to make for me in our pre-vegan days. They were so good, and I was very excited to succeed in recapturing the hearty and flavorful texture with the delicious flavors of veggie sausage and rice. Make sure to use sweet white rice flour in this recipe, as regular rice flour won't work.

Serves 4

2 cups TSP or TVP granules, preferably organic

1½ cups boiling water

½ cup minced fresh parsley, plus more for garnish

3 tablespoons nutritional yeast flakes

1 tablespoon granulated onion

2 teaspoons granulated garlic

1 teaspoon red pepper flakes, or more to taste

1 teaspoon dried oregano

2 teaspoons fennel seeds, lightly crushed with a mortar and pestle

3 tablespoons tamari or soy sauce

4 cloves garlic, minced or pressed

2 cups cooked white rice

¼ cup tomato paste

2 tablespoons sweet white rice flour

4 red or green bell peppers

3½ cups Quick Tomato Basil Sauce (page 185) or store-bought tomato sauce

Preheat the oven to 400°F. Grease a 13 x 9-inch glass or ceramic baking dish.

In a large bowl, combine the TSP and boiling water. Give it a stir, cover with plastic wrap or foil, and let sit for 10 minutes to reconstitute.

To the reconstituted TSP mixture add the parsley, nutritional yeast, granulated onion, granulated garlic, red pepper flakes, oregano, fennel, tamari, fresh garlic, cooked rice, and tomato paste, mixing well. Sprinkle the sweet white rice flour over the mixture and mix well. Using your hands, gently squeeze (but do not mash) the mixture together, which will activate the rice flour to make the mixture stick together.

Slice each pepper in half lengthwise and carefully remove the stem and seeds inside. Pack the filling evenly into each half, mounding the tops as necessary to use all of the filling. Spoon enough sauce into the prepared dish to just cover the bottom. Place the peppers, filling-side up, in a single layer over the tomato sauce.

(recipe continues)

Drizzle more sauce over each pepper. You will probably only have used two-thirds of the sauce at this point. Cover the dish with foil and bake for 40 minutes. Carefully remove the foil. If the peppers aren't tender when pierced with a knife, bake for another 15 minutes. Sprinkle the baked peppers with additional minced fresh parsley.

Heat the remaining sauce and serve on the side.

Chapter Six

• • •

Dessert Casseroles

Baked Coconut Rice Pudding

My kids have such a soft spot in their hearts for rice pudding that we sometimes have it for breakfast instead of dessert. This is a fun new flavor twist on an old-fashioned dessert. It will keep for several days refrigerated and is just as delicious served chilled.

Serves 4 to 6

2 cups water

1 cup medium-grain uncooked sushi rice (such as calrose)

⅔ cup granulated sugar

1 (13.5-ounce) can coconut milk (regular or light)

½ cup plain unsweetened almond milk, soymilk, or other nondairy milk, plus more as needed

Toasted shredded coconut or coconut flakes, for garnish

Preheat the oven to 350°F. Grease an 8-inch square glass or ceramic baking dish.

In a large saucepan over medium heat, combine the water and rice and bring to a boil. Reduce the heat to low, cover, and simmer for 15 minutes. Remove the saucepan from the heat and let sit, covered, for 5 minutes.

Stir the sugar and coconut milk into the cooked rice. Transfer the rice mixture into the prepared baking dish, smoothing the top. Bake for 30 minutes, or until the pudding is thick. Remove from the oven and carefully stir in the almond milk, adding more as needed to thin the pudding to the desired consistency. Scoop the pudding into serving dishes and sprinkle with toasted coconut. The pudding can be served hot or chilled. It will last up to 4 days refrigerated.

Variation: Garnish with some finely chopped candied ginger for a little zing or with sliced fresh mango for extra sweetness.

Old-Fashioned Cinnamon Raisin Rice Pudding

This rice pudding recipe is adapted from my book *Vegan Diner*. One bite of this pudding—with its creamy rice custard, plump raisins, and cinnamon sprinkle—instantly brings me back to childhood. Sometimes you just need something different from the usual suspects of cookies and cake. And sometimes only a bowl of this creamy pudding will do.

Serves 4 to 6

2 cups water

1 cup medium-grain uncooked sushi rice (such as calrose)

½ cup granulated sugar

2 cups plain unsweetened soymilk or almond milk, divided

½ cup raisins

1 teaspoon pure vanilla extract

Ground cinnamon, for garnish

Preheat the oven to 350°F. Grease an 8-inch square glass or ceramic baking dish.

In a large saucepan over medium heat, combine the water and rice and bring to a boil. Reduce the heat to low, cover, and simmer for 15 minutes. Remove the saucepan from the heat and let sit, covered, for 5 minutes.

Stir the sugar, 1½ cups soymilk, raisins, and vanilla into the rice. Transfer the rice mixture into the prepared baking dish, smoothing the top. Bake for 30 minutes, or until the pudding is thick. You will want to give the pudding a little stir after 15 minutes or so. When the pudding is done, remove from the oven and carefully stir in the remaining ½ cup soymilk as needed to keep the pudding from getting too dry. Scoop the pudding into serving dishes and sprinkle with cinnamon. The pudding can be served hot or chilled. It will last up to 2 days refrigerated.

Variation: For a rum-raisin version, stir 2 to 4 tablespoons rum into the baked pudding.

Boysenberry Skillet Crisp

Boysenberry crisp has been a lifelong favorite for my brother and me. When Jon was in college, he would call before he came home for the weekend and beg me to bake him boysenberry crisp. Of course, I always obliged. There's just something about juicy boysenberries baked up with a buttery topping that makes us crazy for this dessert.

Serves 6

FILLING

6 cups fresh or frozen boysenberries
(unthawed if frozen)
⅔ cup granulated sugar
¼ cup plus 5 tablespoons water, divided
¼ cup cornstarch

TOPPING

¾ cup unbleached all-purpose flour
½ cup old-fashioned rolled oats
½ cup firmly packed light brown sugar
1 teaspoon ground cinnamon
¼ cup nonhydrogenated vegan margarine or
coconut oil, melted

FOR THE FILLING

Preheat the oven to 400°F. Grease a 10-inch cast-iron or ovenproof skillet or glass or ceramic pie plate lightly with shortening.

In a saucepan, combine the boysenberries, granulated sugar, and ¼ cup of the water. Bring the mixture to a simmer over medium heat, stirring occasionally.

In a small bowl, whisk together the cornstarch and remaining 5 tablespoons of water until smooth. Stir the cornstarch mixture into the hot berries and simmer until the juices are thick and glossy, for about 5 minutes, stirring continuously.

Remove the saucepan from the heat and scoop the berry mixture into the prepared pan.

FOR THE TOPPING

In a small bowl, mix together the flour, oats, brown sugar, and cinnamon. Add the melted margarine, stirring until incorporated. Using your fingertips, work the margarine into the flour mixture, squeezing until nice and crumbly.

Sprinkle the topping over the boysenberry filling and bake for 15 to 20 minutes, or until the topping is nicely browned.

Gluten-Free: Use gluten-free oats and a gluten-free flour blend without added xanthan gum in place of the all-purpose flour.

Cranberry Apple Crumble

This recipe has been a favorite of mine for many years and is adapted from a recipe by cookbook author Bryanna Clark Grogan. The first time that I met Bryanna, she made this tart and delicious crumble for dessert. Maybe it was the company or the beautiful Denman Island surroundings, but it was one of the best crumbles I've ever had.

Serves 6

FILLING

3 medium-size tart apples, peeled, cored, and cut into ¼-inch slices

3 cups fresh cranberries

1 tablespoon unbleached all-purpose flour or cornstarch

½ cup granulated sugar, or more to taste

TOPPING

¾ cup unbleached all-purpose flour

½ cup old-fashioned rolled oats

½ cup firmly packed light brown sugar

1 teaspoon ground cinnamon

¼ cup coconut oil, nonhydrogenated vegan margarine, or shortening, melted

FOR THE FILLING

Preheat the oven to 375°F. Grease a 9-inch square glass or ceramic baking dish or deep-dish pie plate.

In a medium bowl, gently combine the apples, cranberries, flour, and granulated sugar. Spread the mixture in the prepared pan.

FOR THE TOPPING

In a small bowl, mix together the flour, oats, brown sugar, and cinnamon. Add the melted coconut oil, stirring until incorporated. Using your fingertips, work the oil into the flour mixture, squeezing until nice and crumbly.

Sprinkle the topping over the fruit.

Bake for 40 minutes, or until the apples are soft, the juices are thickened, and the topping is nicely browned.

Remove the crumble from the oven and let it cool on a rack for 20 minutes before serving.

Tip: Serve the crumble warm with a scoop of ice cream.

Gluten-Free: Use cornstarch in the filling and a gluten-free flour blend (without xanthan gum) for the crumble.

Blueberry Peach Skillet Pie

Cast-iron skillets are one of my favorite tools for making and serving pies. I developed this recipe for *The Lodge Cast Iron Cookbook* and have been making it ever since. The combination of blueberries and peaches with a crisp, buttery topping is the best.

Serves 6

FILLING

5 cups frozen blueberries (unthawed)

2 ripe medium peaches, peeled, pitted, and sliced

⅔ cup granulated sugar

¼ cup plus ⅔ cup cool water, divided

¼ cup cornstarch

Grated zest from 1 lemon

TOPPING

1 cup unbleached all-purpose flour

¾ cup old-fashioned rolled oats

¾ cup firmly packed light brown sugar

1 teaspoon freshly grated nutmeg

⅓ cup plus 1 tablespoon nonhydrogenated vegan margarine or coconut oil, melted

Gluten-Free: Use gluten-free oats and a gluten-free flour blend without added xanthan gum in place of the all-purpose flour.

FOR THE FILLING

Preheat the oven to 400°F. Grease a 10-inch cast-iron skillet.

In a large saucepan, combine the blueberries, peaches, granulated sugar, and ¼ cup of the water. Bring to a simmer over medium heat, gently stirring occasionally. Whisk together the cornstarch and remaining ⅔ cup water in a small bowl until smooth. Stir the cornstarch mixture into the hot fruit mixture. Gently stir in the lemon zest, being careful not to mash the peaches. Reduce the heat to medium-low, if necessary, and continue simmering the fruit, gently stirring continuously, until the juices are thick and glossy, about 5 minutes. Remove the saucepan from the heat and carefully scoop the mixture into the prepared skillet.

FOR THE TOPPING

Stir together the flour, oats, brown sugar, and nutmeg in a small bowl. Add the melted margarine, stirring until incorporated. Using your fingertips, work the margarine into the flour mixture, squeezing until nice and crumbly. Sprinkle the topping over the fruit filling.

Bake the pie just until the topping is nicely browned, for 25 to 35 minutes. Serve with ice cream, if you like.

Bumbleberry Cobbler

In my book, you can never have enough berry dessert recipes. Ever! This is another perfect berry dessert to add to your dessert rotation, no matter the season. One of the coolest things about this cobbler is that, even though the berries go on the top, the batter below bakes up into a cake-like topping over them. I adapted this recipe from my pie book, *The Complete Book of Pies*.

Serves 4 to 6

4 cups (1 pound) fresh or frozen mixed berries, such as blueberries, blackberries, and raspberries (unthawed if frozen)

1 cup granulated sugar, divided

1 cup unbleached all-purpose flour

2 teaspoons baking powder

⅛ teaspoon salt

¾ cup plain unsweetened soymilk or other nondairy milk

⅓ cup nonhydrogenated vegan margarine or coconut oil, melted

1 teaspoon pure vanilla extract

Preheat the oven to 350°F. Grease an 11 x 7-inch glass or ceramic baking dish.

In a medium bowl, toss the berries with ¼ cup of the sugar.

In a separate medium bowl, whisk together the flour, baking powder, salt, and remaining ¾ cup sugar. Add the soymilk, melted margarine, and vanilla, whisking to combine.

Scrape the batter into the prepared baking dish. Scoop the berries evenly on top of the batter (don't stir, as the batter will rise to the top as it bakes).

Bake for 65 to 70 minutes, or until the top crust is nicely browned and looks cooked through and the berries have formed a thick sauce. If it looks like there are a few spots where the batter isn't cooked all the way through, which you can confirm by lightly touching the spots with your finger, continue baking for another 5 to 10 minutes, or until fully cooked through. Let the cobbler cool on a rack for 15 minutes before serving.

Gluten-Free: Substitute a mix of ½ cup sorghum flour, ¼ cup superfine brown rice flour, ¼ cup potato starch, and ½ teaspoon xanthan gum for the all-purpose flour.

Nectarine Cobbler

I love to make pies and crisps, but they often need a ton of fresh fruit. I was so excited when I developed this recipe, because not only is it out-of-this-world good but it only uses three nectarines. Although this can serve 4 to 6, my husband almost ate the whole thing. That is my sign of a good dessert. We've probably made it at least fifty times since.

Serves 4 to 6

1 cup unbleached all-purpose flour

2 teaspoons baking powder

⅛ teaspoon salt

¾ cup plus 2 tablespoons granulated sugar, divided

¾ cup plain unsweetened soymilk or other nondairy milk

⅓ cup nonhydrogenated vegan margarine or coconut oil, melted

½ teaspoon almond extract

Grated zest of 1 lemon

3 medium to large nectarines, sliced into wedges

Preheat the oven to 350°F. Grease an 8-inch square glass or ceramic baking dish.

In a large bowl, whisk together the flour, baking powder, salt, and ¾ cup of the sugar. Add the soymilk and melted margarine, whisking to combine. Stir in the almond extract and lemon zest.

Scrape the batter into the prepared baking dish. In a small bowl, toss the nectarines with the remaining 2 tablespoons sugar. Scatter the nectarine slices evenly on top of the batter (don't stir, as the batter will rise to the top as it bakes).

Bake for 55 to 65 minutes, or until the top crust is lightly browned, looks cooked through, and is firm to the touch. Let cool on a rack for 10 minutes before serving.

Gluten-Free: Substitute a mix of ½ cup sorghum flour, ¼ cup superfine brown rice flour, ¼ cup potato starch, and ½ teaspoon xanthan gum for the all-purpose flour.

Cinnamon-Sugar Cheesecake Casserole

Every time my friend Alyssa brings this to a gathering, people literally fight to get some. It's that good! The dessert is a love child between cheesecake and bread pudding, with a cinnamon-sugar crust. Alyssa found the original recipe on Allrecipes.com, which she then changed up and veganized.

Serves 8 to 12

- 3 (8-ounce) containers vegan cream cheese, at room temperature
- 1 cup plus ¾ cup granulated sugar, divided
- 1½ teaspoons pure vanilla extract
- 2 (8-ounce) cans refrigerated vegan crescent roll dough
- 1 teaspoon ground cinnamon
- ½ cup nonhydrogenated vegan margarine, at room temperature
- Agave syrup (optional)

Preheat the oven to 350°F. Grease a 13 x 9-inch glass or ceramic baking dish.

By hand or using a mixer, beat the cream cheese with 1 cup of the sugar and the vanilla in a bowl until smooth.

Unroll one can of the crescent roll dough and press into the bottom of the prepared baking dish, stretching the dough to the edges of the pan. Evenly spread the cream cheese mixture over the dough. Unroll the second can of dough, stretch it out a little bit, and place on top of the cream cheese mixture. Stir together the remaining ¾ cup sugar, the cinnamon, and the margarine. Dot the mixture over the top of the casserole.

Bake for about 30 minutes, or until the dough has puffed up and is golden brown. Remove from the oven and let cool completely in the pan before serving. If desired, you can drizzle the top of the warm casserole with a little agave syrup.

Rustic Bread Pudding

This is comfort food at its very best, and one that I can never get enough of. My grandmother made the best bread pudding, and my recipe is very similar to hers, except that she added dried apricots and raisins. You can definitely choose to add them here.

Serves 4 to 6

½ cup firmly packed light brown sugar

2 tablespoons cornstarch

2¼ cups plain unsweetened soymilk or almond milk

2 tablespoons maple syrup

2 teaspoons pure vanilla extract

5 cups bread cubes (a crusty, rustic bread or French bread is great)

½ cup dairy-free semisweet chocolate chips

½ cup dried cherries

Ground cinnamon, for sprinkling

Preheat the oven to 350°F. Grease an 8-inch square glass or ceramic baking dish.

In a large bowl, whisk together the brown sugar and cornstarch until well blended. Add the soymilk, maple syrup, and vanilla, whisking until smooth. Add the bread cubes and let sit for about 10 minutes, or until the bread is soft and has absorbed most of the milk. Gently fold in the chocolate chips, dried cherries, and a few sprinkles of cinnamon. Don't overmix. Scoop the mixture into the prepared pan. Lightly sprinkle the top with a little more cinnamon.

Bake the pudding for 35 to 45 minutes, or until it is puffed and golden and the milk has been absorbed.

Variation: You can embellish this bread pudding with other additions, such as substituting ½ cup raisins, slivered dried apricots, or chopped toasted hazelnuts for either the chocolate chips or the cherries.

Gluten-Free: Use gluten-free bread cubes.

Chapter Seven

• • •

Sauces, Toppings, and Basics

Crispy Fried Onions

Fried onions may be the must-have topping for green bean casserole, but it seems impossible to find them gluten-free. I thought that crispy onions would be much better homemade anyway, with a crispy rice flour crunch. Once you make these and see how easy they are, you'll want to use them for topping all of your casseroles!

Makes enough to top one 8-inch square casserole

¼ cup white rice flour

2 tablespoons cornstarch

1 small to medium sweet or yellow onion, cut in half and thinly sliced

About ½ cup vegetable oil, for frying

Salt to taste

In a shallow dish, mix together the rice flour and the cornstarch. Sprinkle the sliced onions into the dish and toss with the flour mixture. Heat the oil in a 10-inch cast-iron skillet. Once the oil is very hot, but not smoking, add the onions, a handful at a time in a single layer. Fry the onions until they are light golden brown. Don't cook them beyond this stage, as they will brown further in the oven during baking on top of the casserole. Carefully remove them from the hot oil with tongs or a slotted spoon and place them on paper towels to drain. Sprinkle the onions with a pinch of salt. Repeat with the remaining onions.

Tip: The fried onions should be used the same day that they are made.

Buttery Crumb Topping

A nice buttery crumb topping is my husband's favorite part of a casserole. It is especially good on everything from mac and cheese to vegetable casseroles, as it adds a nice rich, garlicky crunch. Crumb toppings are also open to a number of variations, depending on how you season them.

Makes about ½ cup, enough to top an 8- or 9-inch casserole

½ cup panko breadcrumbs
2 tablespoons nonhydrogenated vegan margarine, melted
1 tablespoon nutritional yeast flakes
1 clove garlic, pressed or finely minced
Pinch of salt

In a small bowl, mix together the panko breadcrumbs, margarine, nutritional yeast, garlic, and a pinch of salt. Adjust seasonings to taste.

Tip: You can substitute olive oil for the margarine, if desired.

Variation: For an herbed-garlic-flavored topping, add 1 tablespoon chopped fresh herbs. For a richer topping, increase the margarine to 3 tablespoons.

Gluten-Free: Use gluten-free panko breadcrumbs. My favorite brand is Ian's, which is also egg-free and dairy-free.

Bakin' Bits

This recipe came from friend and cookbook author Joni Marie Newman. Joni wanted an alternative to the store-bought jars of fake bacon bits, which are vegan but full of hydrogenated fats and dyes. This new-and-improved version makes a perfect addition to casseroles whenever you want a bacon flavor, vegan-style.

Makes about 1 cup

¾ cup plus 2 tablespoons boiling water

¼ teaspoon fine sea salt

2 tablespoons liquid smoke

1 cup TSP or TVP granules, preferably organic

3 tablespoons canola or other neutral-tasting vegetable oil

In a medium saucepan, place the water along with the salt and bring to a boil over medium-high heat. Once boiling, remove the saucepan from the heat.

Add the liquid smoke to the water, mixing well. Add the TSP to the water, stirring well. Cover the saucepan and let stand for 10 minutes.

Preheat a large skillet over medium-high heat and add the oil. Add the reconstituted TSP mixture to the pan and toss to make sure it all gets coated with oil. Pan-fry until the granules reach your desired crispness, stirring them often. You don't necessarily want to brown them, rather you want to dry them out. This should take right around 10 minutes. Allow them to cool completely before transferring to an airtight container. Store in the refrigerator for up to several days.

Smoky Soy Curls

This recipe is adapted from the ever-popular Smoky Curl recipe in *Vegan Diner*. These curls have a smoky and slightly sweet flavor that is a little similar to bacon, but different and delicious in their own right. I love to throw these into casseroles for an extra protein boost. I find myself keeping a batch of these in the fridge for whenever the mood strikes, or just for eating out of hand.

Makes about 4 cups

2 cups boiling water

3 tablespoons low-sodium tamari, divided

2 tablespoons liquid smoke, divided,
  or more to taste

4 ounces dry Soy Curls

¼ teaspoon fine sea salt (optional)

¼ teaspoon freshly ground black pepper, or
  more to taste

1 to 2 tablespoons olive oil, divided, plus more
  as needed

1 tablespoon maple syrup

In a medium bowl, combine the boiling water, 2 tablespoons tamari, and 1 tablespoon liquid smoke. Add the Soy Curls and stir until well mixed. Set aside for 10 minutes, or until the Soy Curls are soft. Transfer them to a colander and drain well, pressing on the Soy Curls to remove the excess liquid. Dry any excess liquid left in the bowl. Return the drained Soy Curls to the bowl and stir in the remaining 1 tablespoon liquid smoke, remaining 1 tablespoon tamari, the salt, if using, and the pepper. Stir until evenly coated.

Preheat a large cast-iron skillet over medium-high heat. Add 1 tablespoon of the oil, coating the bottom of the pan. Add the Soy Curls and cook, stirring every few minutes, for about 10 minutes, or until the Soy Curls are nicely browned. If necessary, reduce the heat to keep them from burning. If you want to make them crispier, add in the additional tablespoon of oil after about 5 minutes. When they are nicely browned and somewhat crispy, drizzle the maple syrup over the curls, tossing them well with a fork, until they are all lightly coated. Cook another minute or two, until slightly caramelized, and remove from the heat.

Use the Smoky Soy Curls in casseroles as needed. You can also cook them for a shorter amount of time for a chewy, softer texture instead of a crispy texture.

Tip: You can add a little more oil when you are cooking them, if needed, or if you want them to be a little richer and crispier. You can also use a vegan pan spray instead of the oil to cook the Soy Curls, if you wish, to keep the fat calories down.

Chicken-Style Soy Curls

Soy Curls, when seasoned just right, make a fantastic chicken substitute. You can cook them up in a skillet to make them chewy, or use them soft and seasoned without any cooking necessary. Either way, simply stir them into a casserole when you want an extra dose of protein or a little cruelty-free deliciousness.

Makes about 4 cups

2 cups boiling water

1 to 2 tablespoons vegan chicken bouillon (powder or paste)

4 ounces dry Soy Curls

3 tablespoons nutritional yeast flakes

1 teaspoon poultry seasoning

1 teaspoon granulated onion

Freshly ground white pepper to taste

1 to 2 tablespoons olive oil, divided

In a medium bowl, combine the boiling water and bouillon to taste. Add the Soy Curls, stirring until mixed. Set aside, stirring occasionally, for 10 minutes, or until the Soy Curls are softened. Transfer them to a colander and drain well, pressing down on the Soy Curls to remove the excess liquid. Dry any excess liquid left in the bowl. Return the drained Soy Curls to the bowl and stir in the nutritional yeast, poultry seasoning, and granulated onion. Add white pepper to taste, stirring well.

To crisp the Soy Curls, preheat a large cast-iron skillet over medium-high heat. Heat 1 tablespoon of the oil. Add the Soy Curls and cook, stirring every few minutes, for 5 minutes, or until the Soy Curls are soft and chewy. If necessary, reduce the heat to keep them from burning, and add in the additional tablespoon of oil if you want to make them crispier. Remove from the heat and use as needed.

Cream of Vegan Chicken Soup

Traditionally, casseroles are often made with cans of store-bought condensed soup. Of course that's no easy task when you're vegan, or even gluten-free. So I did the hard part for you and came up with a homemade version. This recipe is equivalent to one (10.75-ounce) can of condensed cream of chicken soup.

Makes 1 generous cup

1 cup plain unsweetened soymilk or other
    nondairy milk

2 tablespoons raw unsalted cashews,
    soaked for at least 2 hours and drained

2 tablespoons cornstarch

1 teaspoon granulated onion

¾ teaspoon poultry seasoning

2 teaspoons vegan chicken base (such as Better
    Than Bouillon), or more or less to taste

¼ teaspoon granulated garlic

½ teaspoon dried parsley

Dash of freshly ground white or black pepper

In the jar of a blender, combine the soymilk, cashews, cornstarch, onion, poultry seasoning, vegan chicken base, and garlic. Blend until the mixture is super-smooth and no traces of nuts remain. Add the parsley and white pepper and pulse again until mixed.

Pour the mixture into a small saucepan and place over medium heat. Whisk continuously until the sauce mixture comes to a simmer. Reduce the heat slightly to maintain a low simmer and whisk until the sauce is very thick. Remove from the heat.

Use right away, or let cool, whisking occasionally to prevent a skin from forming on the surface. Refrigerate up to 1 day and whisk well before using.

Tip: Some of the recipes in this book may instruct you to double or triple this recipe. Depending on your blender, you may need to blend this in several batches and then cook the batches together in a large saucepan. If you want to serve this as a soup, thin with soymilk to desired thickness. If you're using a high-speed blender, you can skip the soaking step for the cashews and just use them dry. Add a little extra water to blend if needed.

Gluten-Free: Use a gluten-free vegan chicken base.

Cream of Mushroom Soup

This recipe equals one (10.75-ounce) can of condensed mushroom soup. Keep this recipe tucked in your back pocket and use it not only in the recipes in the book, but whenever you need a vegan condensed mushroom soup for your mom's favorite casserole recipes.

Makes about 1 cup

1 cup plain unsweetened soymilk or other nondairy milk

2 tablespoons raw unsalted cashews, soaked for at least 2 hours and drained

2 tablespoons cornstarch

1 teaspoon granulated onion

½ teaspoon granulated garlic

¼ teaspoon dried rubbed sage

½ teaspoon salt

1 cup sliced cremini, baby bella, or button mushrooms, rinsed and patted dry, divided

Freshly ground black pepper to taste

In the jar of a blender, combine the soymilk, cashews, cornstarch, onion, garlic, sage, salt, and half of the mushrooms. Blend until the mixture is super-smooth and no traces of nuts remain. Add the remaining mushrooms and pulse for just a second, until the mushrooms are in smallish chunks. Alternatively, you can dice up the remaining mushrooms by hand, so there's more texture in your sauce. Add pepper to taste.

Pour the blended mixture into a small saucepan and place over medium heat. Whisk continuously until the mixture comes to a simmer. Once the mixture comes to a simmer, reduce the heat slightly to maintain a low simmer, whisking until the sauce is very thick. Remove from the heat.

Use right away, or let cool, whisking occasionally to prevent a skin from forming on the surface. Refrigerate up to 1 day and whisk well before using.

Tip: Some of the recipes in this book may instruct you to double or triple this recipe. Depending on your blender, you may need to blend this in several batches and then cook the batches together in a large saucepan. If you want to serve this as a soup, thin with soymilk to desired thickness. If you're using a high-speed blender, you can skip the soaking step for the cashews and just use them dry. Add a little extra water to blend if needed.

Variation: To make a shiitake mushroom variation, substitute chopped shiitake mushrooms for the same amount of creminis and sauté them for 5 minutes, or until tender, before stirring them into the sauce. Increase the sage to ½ teaspoon, if desired.

Savory Gravy

This fat-free and delicious gravy is adapted from a recipe by Bryanna Clark Grogan. It's not only a key ingredient in a couple of the casseroles in this book, but it also made an appearance in my book *Vegan Diner*. Around our house we affectionately call this "crack gravy."

Makes about 5 cups

⅔ cup nutritional yeast flakes

¼ cup oat flour

½ cup chickpea flour

5 cups cool water

1 tablespoon granulated onion

2 teaspoons granulated garlic

¾ teaspoon dried rubbed sage

2 tablespoons vegan beef bouillon paste
(such as Better Than Bouillon), or to taste

Salt and freshly ground black pepper
to taste

In a heavy, large saucepan over high heat, whisk together the nutritional yeast and flours, cooking until it smells toasty. Pour in the water, whisking until the mixture is smooth. Whisk in the granulated onion, garlic, and sage. Add the bouillon, whisking well. Whisk the gravy constantly over high heat until it thickens and comes to a boil. Reduce the heat to medium-high and simmer for 5 to 10 minutes, or until the gravy is really thick. Adjust the seasonings, adding salt and pepper to taste.

Tip: If you don't have vegan beef bouillon, you can substitute ¼ cup tamari or soy sauce and reduce the water to 4¾ cups. The gravy can be made up to 2 days ahead and refrigerated. Simply reheat in a saucepan, whisking sauce until smooth.

Variation: Substitute 1 cup of pale ale (regular or gluten-free) for 1 cup of the water. You can also swap the dried sage with 2 teaspoons dried dill or 2 tablespoons minced fresh dill (or to taste).

Gluten-Free: Use a gluten-free oat flour and bouillon.

Country-Style Sage Gravy

This is a creamy, sage-infused, thick white country-style gravy. It makes a perfect addition to casseroles and is equally delicious served on the side or on top of casseroles, such as the Thanksgiving Stuffing casserole (page 77). The thickness of the gravy nicely holds all of the casserole ingredients together, and this recipe makes a large enough amount to stir into an entire casserole. If you're just looking for gravy to serve alongside one of the casseroles in this book, thin with additional soymilk or water as needed.

Makes about 3 cups

½ cup oat flour
6 tablespoons nutritional yeast flakes
3¼ cups plain unsweetened soymilk
1 to 1¼ teaspoons dried rubbed sage, depending on how "sage-y" you like it
2½ teaspoons granulated onion
1 teaspoon granulated garlic
1 teaspoon fine sea salt, or more to taste
Freshly ground black pepper to taste

In a large saucepan, whisk together the oat flour and nutritional yeast. Pour in the soymilk, whisking until the mixture is very smooth. Whisk in the sage, granulated onion, garlic, and salt. Add pepper to taste. Place the saucepan over medium-high heat and, whisking continuously, bring to a simmer. Reduce the heat to medium and continue whisking and cooking until the sauce is very thick and smooth, for 5 to 10 minutes. If you are serving this gravy on the side, make the small-batch variation and thin with additional milk or water as needed.

Gluten-Free: Use a gluten-free oat flour and bouillon.

Variation: You can omit the sage in the gravy for a sageless country variation.

Small-Batch Country-Style Sage Gravy

Reduce the oat flour to ⅓ cup, the nutritional yeast flakes to ¼ cup, the soymilk to 2¼ cups, the dried rubbed sage, granulated onion, and fine sea salt to 1 teaspoon each, and the granulated garlic to ¾ teaspoon. Proceed with the large-batch recipe as directed. Season with freshly ground black pepper to taste. Makes about 2¼ cups.

Good Gravy!

This gravy has a delicious, robust flavor, especially if you add a nice dose of freshly ground pepper. It stands up really nicely to cooked macaroni and vegetables in casseroles. If you like beer, definitely try the boozy variation below. If you can find Better Than Bouillon No Beef Base, use it here. It makes all the difference in this gravy. If you're using this gravy not in a casserole but as an accompaniment on the side, you can reduce the oat flour to ⅓ cup, which will give you a thinner gravy.

Makes about 3 cups

½ cup oat flour

6 tablespoons nutritional yeast flakes

3 cups plain unsweetened soymilk

2 teaspoons granulated onion

1 teaspoon granulated garlic

1½ tablespoons vegan beef bouillon paste (such as Better Than Bouillon)

Freshly ground black pepper to taste

In a large saucepan, whisk together the oat flour and nutritional yeast. Whisk in the soymilk until the mixture is very smooth. Whisk in the granulated onion and garlic. Add the bouillon and the pepper to taste, whisking well. Place the saucepan over medium-high heat and, whisking continuously, bring to a simmer. Reduce the heat to medium and continue whisking and cooking until the sauce is very thick and smooth, for 5 to 10 minutes.

Variation: For a delicious boozy version, replace ½ cup soymilk with ½ cup pale ale (regular or gluten-free).

Gluten-Free: Use a gluten-free oat flour and bouillon.

Homemade Chili Powder

For a few years, I've been hearing from friends in Australia that they can't buy chili powder, only hot pepper similar to cayenne. So I set out to create one, as it's an ingredient that I use often in my recipes. What I discovered is that this homemade chili powder tastes so much better than what you buy in the store. Just make sure that your spices are very fresh for the best flavor. I also like to use this mix as a taco seasoning.

Makes about a scant ¾ cup

2 tablespoons sweet paprika

2 tablespoons ground ancho chili powder

2 tablespoons dried oregano

2 tablespoons ground cumin

2 tablespoons granulated garlic

1 tablespoon granulated onion

2 teaspoons fine sea salt

½ teaspoon cayenne pepper

In a small bowl, mix together the paprika, ancho chili powder, oregano, cumin, garlic, onion, salt, and cayenne pepper. Store in an airtight jar and use in recipes whenever chili powder is called for.

Tip: If you can't find ancho chili powder, you can use a total of 4 tablespoons paprika. Don't substitute regular chili powder for the ancho, as it usually is a blend of other spices and not a pure chili powder. If you prefer a lighter cumin flavor, you can reduce the cumin to 2 teaspoons.

Variation: You can add more or less cayenne pepper to the blend. You can also add ground chipotle pepper and/or smoked paprika.

Nacho Cheesy Sauce

I reach for this sauce over and over again. It can be tossed with cooked macaroni, thinned with a little soymilk and drizzled over enchiladas or tacos, or even served up with chips and salsa. However you use it, you can't go wrong. I love to add a nice dose of hot sauce to mine, but that is completely optional.

Makes about 3 cups

3 cups plain unsweetened soymilk or other nondairy milk

6 tablespoons nutritional yeast flakes

½ cup raw unsalted cashews, soaked for at least 2 hours and drained

3 tablespoons oat flour

2 tablespoons cornstarch

2 teaspoons granulated onion

1 teaspoon granulated garlic

1½ teaspoons Homemade Chili Powder (page 175) or store-bought chili powder

1½ teaspoons smoked paprika

1 teaspoon fine sea salt

½ teaspoon ground cumin

Hot sauce or Sriracha (optional)

In the jar of a blender, combine the soymilk, nutritional yeast, cashews, oat flour, cornstarch, granulated onion, garlic, chili powder, paprika, salt, and cumin. Blend the mixture at high speed until completely smooth and no bits of nuts remain. If you don't have a big blender, blend the mixture in two batches.

Transfer the mixture to a large saucepan and place over medium heat. Bring the sauce to a simmer, whisking continuously. Once the mixture comes to a simmer, reduce the heat slightly and cook, whisking continuously until very thick, for 5 to 10 minutes. If desired, add hot sauce and salt to taste.

Tip: If you're using a high-speed blender, you can skip the soaking step for the cashews and just use them dry. Add a little extra water to blend if needed.

Gluten-Free: Use a gluten-free oat flour.

Pub-Style Cream Sauce

I like to mix things up with my sauces, which is what I did with this nice and creamy, boozy beer sauce. It's delicious in the Boozy Baked Penne casserole (page 87) and the Welsh Rarebit Casserole (page 33), or anywhere that you want a creamy, rich, beer-infused sauce. If you have some vegan Cheddar on hand, it's fantastic stirred into the hot sauce, especially if you're making the Welsh Rarebit Casserole (page 33).

Makes about 3 cups

2¼ cups plain unsweetened soymilk or other nondairy milk

¾ cup beer, such as pale ale

6 tablespoons nutritional yeast flakes

3 tablespoons oat flour

2 tablespoons cornstarch

¼ cup raw unsalted cashews, soaked for at least 2 hours and drained

1 teaspoon granulated onion

1 teaspoon fine sea salt, or more to taste

¼ teaspoon freshly grated nutmeg

In the jar of a blender, combine the soymilk, beer, nutritional yeast, oat flour, cornstarch, cashews, granulated onion, salt, and nutmeg. Blend the mixture at high speed until completely smooth. If you don't have a big blender, blend the mixture in two batches.

Transfer the mixture to a large saucepan and place over medium-high heat. Bring the sauce to a simmer, whisking continuously. Once the mixture comes to a simmer, reduce the heat slightly and cook, whisking continuously until the sauce is very thick, for 5 to 10 minutes. Add salt to taste.

Tip: If making this sauce for the Welsh Rarebit Casserole (page 33), add an additional 1 tablespoon of cornstarch to the sauce so that it's thicker and adheres to the bread better. If you're using a high-speed blender, you can skip the soaking step for the cashews and just use them dry. Add a little extra water to blend if needed.

Variation: For a cheesier sauce, stir ¼ to ½ cup shredded vegan Cheddar into the hot sauce until it melts.

Gluten-Free: Use a gluten-free oat flour as well as gluten-free beer.

Cheesy Sauce

I've been playing with different variations of this sauce for a long time. I finally hit on my favorite version. The combination of the oat flour and cornstarch give it just the right body, and the nutritional yeast and seasonings give it a nice cheesy flavor. Although you may be tempted to substitute tapioca starch for the cornstarch, don't. I've tried, and it just doesn't come out as well. If using this sauce to drizzle over a casserole, thin with additional soymilk as needed.

Makes about 3 cups

3 cups plain unsweetened soymilk

⅓ cup raw unsalted cashews, soaked for at least 2 hours and drained

8 tablespoons nutritional yeast flakes

3 tablespoons oat flour

2 tablespoons cornstarch

1¼ teaspoons fine sea salt, or more to taste

1 teaspoon smoked paprika

1 teaspoon granulated onion

1 teaspoon Sriracha (optional)

In the jar of a blender, combine the soymilk, cashews, nutritional yeast, oat flour, cornstarch, salt, paprika, granulated onion, and Sriracha, if using. Blend the mixture at high speed until completely smooth and no bits of nuts remain. If you don't have a big blender, blend the mixture in two batches.

Transfer the mixture to a large saucepan and place over medium-high heat. Bring the sauce to a simmer, whisking continuously. Once the mixture comes to a simmer, reduce the heat slightly and cook, whisking continuously until thickened, for 5 to 10 minutes.

Tip: If you're using a high-speed blender, you can skip the soaking step for the cashews and just use them dry. Add a little extra water to blend if needed.

Variation: To make this a white cheesy sauce without the smokiness, omit the smoked paprika and the Sriracha.

Gluten-Free: Use a gluten-free oat flour.

Almost Alfredo Sauce

Although this isn't exactly a true alfredo sauce with loads of cream and butter, it is an all-purpose creamy white sauce, which works really well in so many recipes. There are a number of variations for it, from adding truffle oil to white wine. It's so versatile, that it may just become your new secret sauce.

Makes about 3 cups

2½ cups plain unsweetened soymilk
½ cup water
½ cup raw unsalted cashews, soaked for at least 2 hours and drained
2 tablespoons nutritional yeast flakes
3 tablespoons oat flour
2 tablespoons cornstarch
1¼ teaspoons fine sea salt, or more to taste
1 teaspoon granulated onion

In the jar of a blender, combine the soymilk, water, cashews, nutritional yeast, oat flour, cornstarch, salt, and granulated onion. Blend the mixture at high speed until completely smooth and no bits of nuts remain. If you don't have a big blender, blend the mixture in two batches.

Transfer the mixture to a large saucepan and place over medium-high heat. Bring the sauce to a simmer, whisking continuously. Once the mixture comes to a simmer, reduce the heat slightly and cook, whisking continuously until thickened, for 5 to 10 minutes.

Tip: Use a good-tasting unsweetened soymilk for this sauce, as the flavor really comes through. If you're using a high-speed blender, you can skip the soaking step for the cashews and just use them dry. Add a little extra water to blend if needed.

Variations:
To make a truffle sauce, to the blender jar add 1 to 3 tablespoons truffle oil to taste and reduce the granulated onion to ½ teaspoon. Add a few sprinkles of freshly grated nutmeg.

To make a white wine sauce, replace ¾ cup of soymilk with an equal amount of white wine.

To make this sauce lower in fat, reduce the cashews to ⅓ cup.

Gluten-Free: Use a gluten-free oat flour.

Creamy Tahini Sauce

When you make a sauce out of tahini and water, it gets remarkably thick and creamy, especially after it sits for a little while. It also has a nice roasted flavor, which pairs well with some of the Mediterranean recipes in this book, like the Chickpeas with Rice, Dill, and Tomatoes (page 128). If you make the sauce ahead of time, you may need to thin it out with a little additional water.

Makes about a scant 1¼ cups

⅓ cup sesame tahini (preferably roasted, as it has much more flavor)

⅔ cup warm water

2 tablespoons freshly squeezed lemon juice

2 cloves garlic, pressed or minced

¼ teaspoon ground cumin

¼ teaspoon salt

In a blender, add the tahini, water, lemon juice, garlic, cumin, and salt. Blend until smooth and creamy. Refrigerate the sauce until ready to use, up to 3 days.

Salsa Fresca

Homemade salsa is a perfect accompaniment to casseroles, especially enchiladas (see page 135 and page 137) and the Bean and Rice Casserole (page 67). It also happens to be one of the easiest recipes to make. It's simply a matter of tossing a few ingredients into the food processor and pulsing until combined. Once you realize how easy it is, you'll be making this all of the time. You can even customize it to your particular tastes, including heat level: if you want a milder salsa, seed the jalapeño first and/or use less than called for in the recipe.

Makes about 2 cups

½ jalapeño, stemmed (optional)
¼ small yellow onion
½ large bunch cilantro leaves, rinsed and
     patted dry
1 (14.5-ounce) can diced tomatoes, preferably
     organic and fire-roasted, undrained
Chipotle powder or smoked paprika to taste
Freshly squeezed lime juice (optional)
Salt to taste

In the bowl of a food processor fitted with the metal blade, place the jalapeño, if using, and onion and cilantro and pulse just until diced. Add the tomatoes, pulsing until combined. Don't over-process the salsa into a smooth sauce.

Place the salsa in a bowl. Stir in the chipotle powder. Add a dash or two of fresh lime juice to taste, if using. Add salt to taste, stirring well. This salsa is best served the day that it is made.

Tip: If you don't have a food processor, you can make this by hand. Just swap fresh tomatoes for the canned, dice the jalapeño, onion, and tomatoes, mince the cilantro, and mix all of the ingredients together in a bowl.

Variation: Substitute a couple large beefsteak or heirloom tomatoes for the canned.

Everyday Enchilada Sauce

For years I've been trying to come up with a quick and easy enchilada sauce that's full of flavor. I would often reach for canned sauce because it was easy and it tasted, well, like enchiladas. But once you try your hand at homemade enchilada sauce, you'll never go back to canned again.

Makes about 4 cups

2 cups cool water

1 (14.5-ounce) can diced tomatoes, preferably organic, undrained

3 tablespoons tomato paste

2 tablespoons plus 2 teaspoons Homemade Chili Powder (page 175) or store-bought chili powder

1 teaspoon ground cumin

2 cloves garlic, pressed or finely minced

1 teaspoon granulated onion

1 teaspoon dried oregano

1 teaspoon fine sea salt, or more to taste

2 tablespoons canola oil

⅛ teaspoon xanthan gum

In a blender, combine the water, tomatoes, tomato paste, chili powder, cumin, garlic, onion, oregano, salt, and canola oil. Blend until smooth. Add the xanthan gum and blend again until smooth. Adjust the seasonings to taste.

Tip: Although you may be tempted to omit the oil from this recipe, it really helps to round out the flavors of the spices.

The xanthan gum works as a thickener and emulsifier in this recipe. You only want that tiny bit, which works like magic. Look for xanthan gum in the gluten-free aisle in your local grocery store or online.

Quick Tomato Basil Sauce

This is a lovely all-purpose tomato sauce that you can use in any of the recipes in this book that call for tomato sauce. The sauce will last about 5 days refrigerated and can be frozen for longer storage.

Makes about 4 cups

1 (28-ounce) can diced, plum, or San Marzano tomatoes, preferably organic, undrained

1 (6-ounce) can tomato paste

2 to 3 cloves garlic

1 teaspoon dried oregano

2 to 3 teaspoons granulated sugar

8 to 10 fresh basil leaves, very thinly sliced, divided

1 teaspoon fine sea salt, or more to taste

Gluten-Free

In the jar of a blender, combine the tomatoes, tomato paste, garlic, oregano, and sugar. Blend until smooth. Add half of the basil to the blender and briefly blend with a couple of quick bursts until the basil is finely chopped into bits but not puréed. Add the salt to taste.

Transfer to a saucepan and bring the mixture to a simmer over medium heat. Reduce the heat to low, cover the sauce, and simmer for 10 minutes. Stir in the remaining basil. Sauce will keep refrigerated for several days.

Variation: For a richer sauce, add 1 to 2 tablespoons olive oil and blend with the tomatoes.

Cornbread

I've been making this recipe for many years, and I discovered that it also makes the ultimate casserole topping. Try it in the Sloppy Joe Cornbread Casserole (page 75) or the Old-Fashioned Tamale Pie (page 81). You can't go wrong! This recipe can also be made gluten-free too. If you're using it as a topping, the recipe makes enough to top one 8-, 9-, or 10-inch casserole. If baking this as a regular pan of cornbread, bake it in an 8-inch square pan.

Serves 6

¾ cup fine or medium-grind yellow cornmeal

¾ cup unbleached all-purpose flour

2 tablespoons granulated sugar

2 teaspoons baking powder

¼ teaspoon fine sea salt

1 cup plain soymilk or other nondairy milk

3 tablespoons canola oil

One of my favorite brands of cornmeal comes from Bob's Red Mill.

Preheat the oven to 400°F. Grease an 8-inch square glass or ceramic baking dish with shortening.

In a large bowl, mix together the cornmeal, flour, sugar, baking powder, and salt. Add the soymilk and oil to the flour mixture, stirring just until combined. Be careful not to overmix the batter.

If using the batter for a casserole topping, spread it over the top of the casserole and bake according to the recipe directions. If baking it as a regular pan of cornbread, scoop the batter into the prepared pan. Bake for 30 to 40 minutes, or until the cornbread is lightly browned on top and a tester inserted into the center comes out clean. Baking times may vary slightly depending on the pan you use.

Remove the cornbread from the oven and set aside to cool until ready to serve.

Gluten-Free: Substitute the all-purpose flour with ½ cup sorghum flour, ¼ cup tapioca starch/flour, and ½ teaspoon xanthan gum. You will also need to add an additional ¼ cup of nondairy milk.

Flaky Pie Dough

This recipe makes a great flaky pastry, perfect for topping your pot pies or casseroles. If you're making a really large casserole, you can double the recipe. This recipe was first published in *The Complete Book of Pies*, and I couldn't resist using it in my book *Vegan Diner* as well.

Makes 1 crust

1½ cups unbleached all-purpose flour

¼ teaspoon sea salt

½ cup nonhydrogenated vegetable shortening, chilled

3 to 5 tablespoons ice water

Plain unsweetened soymilk or almond milk, for brushing

In the bowl of a food processor fitted with a metal blade, combine the flour and salt, pulsing until mixed. Add the shortening, pulsing just until the mixture resembles a coarse meal.

Add 3 tablespoons ice water to the flour mixture, pulsing until moist clumps form, stopping to test the dough with your fingertips to see if it's moist enough to hold together. If the dough is too dry, add another tablespoon or two of ice water, as needed. Remove the blade and gather the dough into a ball, then flatten it into a disk. Wrap in plastic wrap and chill for at least 30 minutes.

Roll the dough out into the shape of your casserole dish, leaving a little extra overhang for crimping the edges. Place the dough on top of your casserole and crimp or press the edges into the inside edge of the casserole dish. Using a sharp knife, cut a few slits into the center of the dough so that the steam can vent while baking. Brush the top of the dough with a little soymilk and bake according to the casserole directions.

Tip: I like to use nonhydrogenated vegetable shortening because it's a much healthier choice.

SOURCES

Ancient Harvest
www.quinoa.net
Manufacturer of delicious quinoa pasta
and prepared polenta that work really well in
the casserole recipes.

Authentic Foods
www.authenticfoods.com
Manufacturer of superfine gluten-free flours.
Their superfine rice flours are a must-have for
gluten-free baking.

Beyond Meat
www.beyondmeat.com
Manufacturer of Beyond Meat vegan
chicken products. Their products are gluten-free
too.

Bob's Red Mill Natural Foods ·
www.bobsredmill.com
(800) 349-2173
A fantastic source for whole grain flours,
grains, and beans.

Cuisinart
www.cuisinart.com
Manufacturer of small kitchen appliances and
cookware, including food processors, mixers,
and ice cream makers.

DeBoles
www.deboles.com
Manufacturer of my favorite gluten-free no-boil
lasagna noodles.

Ian's
www.iansnaturalfoods.com
Manufacturer of gluten-free and vegan panko
breadcrumbs. They are worth seeking out to use
in casseroles if you're gluten-free.

KitchenAid
www.kitchenaid.com
Manufacturer of both small and large kitchen
appliances, including food processors, mixers,
and ranges.

Le Creuset

www.lecreuset.com

Manufacturer of excellent-quality casserole dishes and Dutch ovens, enameled cast-iron cookware, ceramic pie plates, mixing bowls, silicone spatulas, and much more.

Lodge

www.lodgemfg.com

(423) 837–7181

Manufacturer of excellent-quality American-made cast-iron skillets, enameled Dutch ovens, casserole dishes, and more.

Nielsen-Massey Vanillas

www.nielsenmassey.com

(847) 578–1550

Manufacturer of high-quality pure vanilla extracts, beans, and powders, as well as a variety of other pure extracts.

Red Star

www.redstaryeast.com

My favorite manufacturer of nutritional yeast flakes.

Soy Curls

www.butlerfoods.com

(503) 879–5005

Manufacturer of Soy Curls, a dry product made from the whole soybean.

Superior Touch

www.superiortouch.com/retail/products/better -than-bouillon/vegetarian-bases

Manufacturer of Better Than Bouillon vegetarian/vegan beef and chicken bouillons, which are fantastic in sauces and casseroles.

Sweet & Sara Vegan Marshmallows

www.sweetandsara.com

Sara makes the most amazing vegan marshmallows, which are a perfect topping for sweet casseroles. They are available on her website, as well as in upscale and vegan grocery stores.

Tinkyada

www.tinkyada.com

Manufacturer of gluten-free brown rice pasta. Their pastas are excellent and hold up well in these casseroles.

INDEX

Note: Page references in *italics* indicate photographs.